Wonderful

Normandy

Text **René Gaudez**

Photography **Hervé Hughes**

Translation **id2m**

Editions OUEST-FRANCE

LA MANCHE
0
30 km
BAIE DE LA SEINE
CÔTE DE NACRE
Nez de Jobourg
Beaumont-Hague
Jobourg
Équeurdreville-Hainneville
Cherbourg
Saint-Pierre-Eglise
Pointe de Barfleur
Barfleur
St-Vaast-la-Hougue
Valognes
Bricquebec
St-Sauveur-le-Vicomte
Ste-Mère-Église
Barneville-Carteret
Isigny-sur-Mer
Carentan
La Haye-du-Puits
Arromanche
Courseulles
Bayeux
Ouistreham
50
Lessay
St-Clair-sur-l'Elle
Balleroy
Tilly-sur-Seulles
Périers
Vire
Saint-Lô
St-Sauveur-Lendelin
Torigni-sur-Vire
Villers-Bocage
Agon-Coutainville
Coutances
Pointe d'Agon
Tessy-s-Vire
MANCHE
14
Îles Chausey
Pointe du Roc
Granville
St-Sever-Calvados
Vire
Condé-sur-Noireau
Falaise
Villedieu-les-Poêles
Tinchebray
Athis-de-l'Orne
Orne
61
Baie du Mont-Saint-Michel
Avranches
Sourdeval
Flers
Le Mont-St-Michel
Juvigny-le-Tertre
Mortain
Domfront
Pontorson
Sélune
St-Hilaire-du-Harcouët
La Ferté-Macé
St-James

Mers-les-Bains
Le Tréport
Eu
Blangy-sur-Bresle
Dieppe
Varengeville-sur-Mer
St-Valery-en-Caux
Veulettes-sur-Mer
CÔTE D'ALBÂTRE
Bresle
Béthune
Fécamp
Cany-Barville
76
Neufchâtel-en-Bray
Aumale
Yport
Étretat
Cap d'Antifer
Doudeville
Fauville-en-Caux
Yerville
Tôtes
St-Saëns
Goderville
Yvetot
SEINE-MARITIME
Forges-les-Eaux
Le Havre
Bolbec
Caudebec-en-Caux
Barentin
Cap de la Hève
ROUEN
Andelle
Gournay-en-Bray
Quillebeuf
CÔTE FLEURIE
Honfleur
Risle
Seine
Le Petit-Quevilly
Le Grand-Quevilly
St-Étienne-du-Rouvray
Lyons-la-Forêt
Deauville
Trouville-sur-Mer
Cabourg
Touques
Pont-Audemer
Étrépagny
Gisors
Pont-l'Évêque
Elbeuf
Blangy-le-Château
Les Andelys
Louviers
Brionne
Cambremer
Lisieux
27
Le Neubourg
Iton
Seine
Epte
Mézidon-Canon
Gaillon
Vernon
St-Pierre-sur-Dives
Bernay
Beaumont-le-Roger
Eure
Giverny
Orbec
Évreux
Touques
Broglie
Pacy-sur-Eure
Livarot
EURE
Vimoutiers
Conches-sur-Ouche
Risle
Trun
La Ferté-Frênel
Breteuil
Damville
Ivry-la-Bataille
Eure
Argentan
Gacé
L'Aigle
Nonancourt
Risle
Iton
ORNE
Avre
Verneuil-sur-Avre
Mortrée
Moulins-la-Marche
Sées
Tourouvre
Mortagne-au-Perche
Longny-au-Perche
Alençon
Le Mêle-sur-Sarthe
Sarthe
Bellême
Nocé
Le Theil

Normandy, a duchy and rural land

Normandy was founded in 911 when Charles the Simple, the then King of France, signed the Treaty of Saint-Clair-sur-Epte and consequently ceded territory in the lower Seine valley to Rollo, a Viking of Norwegian origin. William Longsword and William the Conqueror, Rollo's descendants, then extended the borders of this duchy to form modern-day Normandy, and though short-lived, this memorable duchy contributed hugely to the heritage of the region. In 1204, the King of France, Philippe Auguste, seized the duchy and, following its occupation by the English during the Hundred Years' War, Louis XI put an end to its existence in 1469.

Normandy stretches over 11,500 square miles and is divided into five *départements* – Seine-Maritime and Eure, which form Haute-Normandie, and Calvados, Orne and Manche, which together make up Basse-Normandie. Geographers, historians and even tourist boards have also created innumerable *pays*, or areas, whose origins and borders are often uncertain, including Caux, Bray, Roumois,

Left

Having seized Château-Gaillard in Les Andelys, Philippe Auguste incorporated the duchy into the Kingdom of France.

Ouche, Auge, Hièmois, Perche, Bessin and Cotentin. Normandy's only natural borders are formed by the sea, and, for a few miles to the east and the south, rivers including the Bresle, the Epte, the Avre, the Eure and the Sarthe. The region also boasts very diverse landscapes, including plains, groves, forests, riverbanks and cliff faces. Even the houses differ in style due to the many different materials used (wood timbering, limestone, granite, schist, millstone and bricks, slate and tiles). Industrial Normandy in the Seine valley contrasts agricultural Normandy further west. Famous for its milk and apples, it also produces cereal, flax, beetroot and early fruit and vegetables. Cows are a familiar sight in the region but Basse-Normandie, in particular, has always been horse country. Given its diversity, it is hard to sum up Normandy in a few words but one thing is certain – the lush pastures and meadows owe much of their beauty to the welcome rain showers.

Nature has blessed the region with magnificent places of interest, including Etretat, the Val de Seine, Marais Vernier marsh, La Hague peninsula, the Bay of Mont-Saint-Michel and the Swiss Normandy area. And history has created even more, for example Saint-Vaast-la-Hougue, Cocherel, Ivry and Granville provided the setting for distant battles that are remembered in the history books. The Battle of Normandy turned the pastures into vast cemeteries and the people of the region paid heavily for the Liberation of Europe. During the Renaissance period, many sailors set off from Honfleur, Dieppe and other Normandy ports to discover the world.

Normandy is also a pious land. It is dotted with sanctuaries and abbeys dedicated to either Our Lady or Saint Michel. Built during the time of the dukes and then entrusted to the Benedictine order, some are still places of worship and many are architectural masterpieces. Thérèse Martin, St. Theresa of the Child Jesus, made Lisieux a world pilgrimage centre.

But Normandy probably boasts more castles than monasteries. Though less famous than the ones that stand majestically on the river Loire, Normandy's castles are just as beautiful if not more diverse in style.

From Corneille to Salacrou, Fontenelle and Alexis de Tocqueville to Alain, from Bernardin de Saint-Pierre, Barbey d'Aurevilly, Flaubert and Maupassant to Proust, Maurois and Gide, not forgetting modern-day writers Patrick Grainville, Annie Ernaux and Philippe Delerm, few regions can claim to have fathered or captured the hearts of so many playwrights, thinkers, poets and writers. And Normandy continues to attract all kinds of artists. Whether they were born in the region like Géricault, Boudin, Millet and Dufy or they simply set up their easels there, numerous artists look to Normandy for inspiration.

And Normandy holds something for everyone. Lovers of the Gallo-Roman period should head for Le Vieil-Evreux in the Eure, Lillebonne in Seine-Maritime or Vieux-la-Romaine in Calvados, those seeking lace, ironwork, pottery or ivory objects should set off for Rouen, Bayeux, Alençon, Argentan and Dieppe, and those fascinated by technical wizardry and great engineering works should plan days out in Le Havre, Tancarville and Cherbourg.

Varengeville, Harcourt, Saint-Christophe-le-Jajolet and Vauville are known for their parks and gardens and Le Pin and Saint-Lô for their horses. Finally, Deauville, Cabourg, Coutances and Dieppe are the places to go for cinema, jazz or even kite flying! And these are just a few ideas. As for regional cuisine, tripe from Caen, sole *à la dieppoise*, duckling *à la rouennaise*, Vire *andouille* chitterling sausage or Mortagne black pudding are just some of the specialities that, along with cream, cheese, cider and calvados, have made Normandy famous for its gastronomy. The region's markets and fairs, crowded, lively and picturesque, are an explosion of rich, colourful local fare.

Bernstam's statue of Gustave Flaubert, Place des Carmes in Barentin.

Manche

The *département* of the Manche takes its name from the Manche or English Channel - the stretch of water that has carved out three of its borders. Its 220 miles of coastline, stormed to the west by the strongest tides in Europe, long ago confirmed its maritime vocation.

Many of its 482,000 inhabitants also rely on agriculture for their livelihood. The lush green *département* of the Manche is far from industrial but the La Hague peninsula is a major nuclear site, supplying 4% of France's energy. The farthest west of Normandy's *départements*, it stretches over 93 miles from north to south and is a land of contrasts. Its 2,475 square miles are crisscrossed with wooded hills, marshes, heathland and groves but surprisingly it is the *département* with the fewest trees in France.

Given its never-ending coastline and close proximity to England, it served as a stronghold and many of its towns are perched up high for protection. As far back as the Gallic Wars, one of Caesar's lieutenants fought off the people of Gaul here. Two thousand years later, the Manche was the scene of some of the most violent fighting during the Battle of Normandy.

Left
Mont-Saint-Michel, "[...] this gigantic granite jewel, which is as light in its effect as a bit of lace and is covered with towers, with slender belfries [...]", Maupassant, The Horla.

Abbeys are more frequent here than elsewhere, some nestle in the heart of peaceful valleys while the most famous stands at the mercy of the sea.

AVRANCHES

If you are arriving from Brittany or the Maine region, explore the Manche from Mortain, which stands on the banks of the Cance. Visit the *Abbaye Blanche*, or White Abbey, which takes its name from the white habits of its first nuns and marvel at the *Chrismale*, a mysterious reliquary on display in the Church of Saint-Evroult. Paths lead to the *Grande* and *Petite Cascade* waterfalls, the *Fosse-Arthour* (a site evoking Arthurian legend), *Aiguille de Mortain* peak or a hilltop boasting an incredible view from Passais to the *Pointe du Grouin*. This hilltop bears a memorial to the American soldiers who fought the 7th German army here in July 1944. In Ducey, the castle, home to the Montgommery family, stands on the banks of the river Sélune.

The old streets of Avranches – a sub-prefecture of the Manche – tower over the river Sée and lead to the castle, its keep, the Episcopal palace which is now the town's museum, and the former Abbey of Sainte-Anne-de-Moutons.

The town has close links with nearby Mont-Saint-Michel. Maupassant described the view of the bay and abbey from the public gardens. The Church of Saint-Gervais-Saint-Protais' treasure house holds Saint Aubert's skull, which was pierced by Archangel Michael's finger. The recently-opened Scriptorial enables visitors to admire several of the 400 Mont-Saint-Michel manuscripts, some of which are wonderfully illuminated. These were once kept in the Abbey library, whose 14,000 works were rescued by the town of Avranches. This collection and museum are unique in the world.

Top of page
A superb example of Romanesque architecture, Mortain.

Left
The *Abbaye Blanche* in Mortain and the cloister.

Right page
Avranches citadel's keep, built in the 10th century on the remains of the Roman enclosure. The flags sum up the history of the town well.

MONT-SAINT-MICHEL

Of all Normandy's outstanding sights, Mont-Saint-Michel – a UNESCO world heritage site – is the most famous. Often referred to as the "Wonder of the West", its pyramid-shaped silhouette is known throughout the world.

This site has generated many legends that have since been disproved by historians and archaeologists. It is said that the sea turned Mount Tombe into an island after having swallowed up the forest of Scissy that used to encircle it. Even the history of the monastery remains much debated today.

Tradition has it that in 709, Bishop Aubert of Avranches dedicated an oratory to Saint Michel at the top of the mount (the site having already been used by the Celts to honour their gods).

Three centuries later, the Dukes of Normandy drove out the canons, who had been introduced by Aubert, replacing them instead with Benedictine monks. The monks built an initial church with two naves (Notre-Dame-sous-Terre) but this was soon replaced by a second at the top of the mount. For years, however, the area was nothing more than a building site. Granite arrived regularly from the Chausey Islands and the site was overrun with all kinds of craftsmen.

The abbey church was built in the 11th and 12th centuries and the *Merveille* or Wonder buildings (designed to house the monks and visiting pilgrims) followed in the early 13th century. The abbot's house, administrative buildings and garrison came later and by this time the abbey had been turned into a fortress. A row of ramparts, running from *Tour Gabriel* to *Tour Boucle*, protected its base and a small yet powerful fort-like castle guarded its gate.

During the Hundred Years' War, the abbey was therefore able to ward off attacks from the English, who had set up camp on the island of Tombelaine, and, during the Wars of Religion, it drove back the Protestants. Du Guesclin and Louis d'Estouteville were the most famous of the garrison's captains.

Its influence began to wane towards the end of the Middle Ages and only a dozen or so monks remained on the eve on the French Revolution. Louis XI set up his famous "iron cages" here and Napoleon turned the site into a

Below
Made into a stronghold in the 13th century, Mont-Saint-Michel abbey was able to resist all attacks.

prison where successive regimes imprisoned both opponents and common law criminals until 1863. The abbey was falling into disrepair when it was entrusted to the *Monuments historiques*, or listed building commission, for restoration in 1873. The addition of the spire – which, at 157 metres above sea level, crowns Frémiet's statue of Archangel Michael bringing down the devil – marked the renaissance of the abbey in 1897 and gave the Mount its lasting image. The Benedictine order, which had returned to the monastery in 1969, recently left again and has been replaced by the Jerusalem Community, which now provides a spiritual presence and welcomes pilgrims. The last remaining Benedictine monks left as they were unable to find peace and meditate – every year three to four million people flock to the Mont-Saint-Michel, drawn by the majesty and originality of the site or the history and beauty of the monastery rather than by religious belief.

No sooner had the abbey been founded than a village grew up at its foot and the small town of Mont-Saint-Michel is now home to a hundred or so inhabitants or *Miquelots*. The *Porte de l'Avancée* (the only gate open along the ramparts) and *Porte du Roi* provide access to the steep and narrow cobbled *Grande Rue* or Main Street, which is dotted with gift shops and restaurants. It leads to the museums, the *Archéoscope* multimedia show, the *Logis Tifaine* (Du Guesclin's house), the parish church and its magnificent statue of St. Michael and ends at the *Grand Degré* – the first steps in the climb towards the abbey.

The visible platform to the west bears witness to the technical feat involved in building the abbey. As the top of the Mount was too narrow for such a building, a huge slab of rock was added. The church now stands on this slab, supported by three crypts, including the *Gros Piliers* crypt. Inside the church, the elegance and luminosity of the chancel contrast the simplicity of the more sombre nave. Both were built during the same period but over the centuries the Mount was plagued by fire and neglect. The Romanesque chancel collapsed and was rebuilt in the Flamboyant style.

Similarly, in the 17th century, the Maurists pulled down three of the

Above

These sought-after salt meadow lambs graze on the grasses of the bay, but major work is underway to give the Mount back its island status.

Below
The abbey is first and foremost a place of prayer and the Jerusalem Community welcomes visitors.

nave's bays and built a classical façade as they did not have the means to restore it in its original style.

Every period has left its mark and the architects and sculptors of the Middle Ages paid particular attention to detail. At least this is the impression you get when you visit the abbey, its sanctuaries and the *Merveille* buildings - *Salle des Chevaliers*, *Salle des Hôtes*, the refectory – with its surprising lighting and acoustics – and the cloister whose arcade alone is a work of art.

The view from the gardens, parapet walk and ramparts stretches far across the bay and, steeped in legend, this vista is just as renowned as the monastery itself. At low tide, when the sun is just peeping over the horizon, the silhouette of the Mount can be made out in the expanse of shimmering mud and sand that is lined with grasses and criss-crossed by rivers and channels. Clouds float by and birds, those flecks in the sky, complete the palette of colours. Visit one of the *Maisons de la baie* and find out more about life in the bay, its plants, wildlife and quicksand, and the extensive efforts being made to stop it silting up, in particular the replacement of the sea wall which leads to the Mount with a walkway and system of public transport and the removal of the car parks which spoil the approach. Hang on! Soon the sea will wash over as much as 7 miles of land and reclaim its territory. It may even surround the Mount. Does the tide really come in as fast as a galloping horse? Let's just say that it comes in fast enough to catch out several ill-informed tourists each year who owe their lives to the quick-thinking emergency services.

Right page
" [...] Mont St. Michel which is to the ocean what the Pyramid of Cheops is to the desert." Victor Hugo, *Ninety-Three.*

GRANVILLE

The route between saint-jean-le-thomas and carolles, on the road from Genêts to Granville, is considered by some to be the most beautiful in France. To discover the Thar valley, turn off this route. Set in majestic parkland, the monastic buildings of the Abbey of Lucerne-d'Outre-Mer have been perfectly restored thanks to the patient work of Abbot Lelégard.

Granville, known as the Monaco of the North because of its resemblance to the Principality, made its wealth from the sea. Its seamen manned fast ships bound for Newfoundland and fished several miles out for wild oysters or the specially cultivated oyster, *pied de cheval*. Today they fish for clams. The beach at Plat Gousset has been popular with bathers since the 19th century. Nowadays, fishing, yachting and sea water therapy provide most of its income.

Threaded among the ramparts, stairways and cobbled paths lead to the *Haute Ville*, or old town. At the entrance to the town, a plaque commemorates the assault of the proroyalist people of Vendée on the people of Granville in 1793, who routed them before turning to fight the flames lit by the would-be invaders. The museum of Vieux-Granville explores this past. The town boasts a 15th-century church – whose miraculous statue of Notre-Dame-du-Cap-Lihou was brought out to bless seafarers – former barracks built in the 18th and 19th centuries, the *maison du guet*, or watchtower, and fine mansions built in former times by privateers and shipowners. Narrow alleys lead to the *Roc*, the lighthouse and signal station.

The *Haute Ville* is also home to the *Musée Richard-Anacréon*, a Granville native whose bequest enabled its creation. Granville counts the fashion designer Christian Dior among its famous citizens. He was born here in 1905 and his villa "Les Rhumb's" is now a museum, the only one in France devoted to a top fashion designer. The town was founded by the English. During the Hundred Years' War, they bought a few acres of land on the *Roc* to build a fortress but were soon driven out by Louis d'Estouteville, captain of the Mont-Saint-Michel. But not before they had the time to dig the "English Trench", which provides access to the beach from the harbour area.

Right page

From the harbour in Granville, pedestrian walkways and stairways lead to the "haute ville" where most of the town's architectural heritage is situated. Jules Michelet wrote *La Mer* in this town.

Above

The tide has emptied the docks of its fishing fleet. Perched over the quays, the ramparts, disused barracks and the characteristic silhouette of the Church of Notre-Dame-du-Cap-Lihou.

CH 846675
CH 347520

THE CHAUSEY ISLANDS

From Granville, hop aboard a boat bound for Chausey, which is in the town's administrative area. Nine nautical miles out to sea, these fifty-two islands that have never been submerged form Normandy's only archipelago. "Forgotten" in the treaty of Brétigny, the islands remained French and thus are not part of the Channel Islands.

This unique place has played host to visitors since prehistoric times. Shapes, colours and surfaces shift with the tide, which has a range of 14 metres. Maîtresse Ile, at just over a mile long and no wider than 800 metres, is the only inhabited island. A few people live here all year round, several hundred in summer. There are no cars or even bicycles in this paradise. The main buildings of interest on the publicly-owned part of the island are the lighthouse, a fort dating from 1866, hotels, a few villas, a pyramid that serves as a sea mark and the former presbytery and school. On the privately owned part, which is, however, open to the public, the path wends its way past the house of artist and navigator Marin Marie, a chapel, an old farm, a few house clusters – called "Ville", "Blainvillais" and "Le Pont" – and on past a castle rebuilt by Louis Renault. It then leads to two fine beaches and to the signal station which, long fallen into disuse, has recently been restored and has once again been able to receive signals to its mast, bringing back to life the images seen on old postcards. Sites such as the Spear (l'Epée), the Monks (les Moines) and the Elephant are named after the peculiar shapes of rocks. Around Grande Ile, low tide uncovers over 5,000 hectares of sand banks and 365 tiny islands, blackened with seaweed and linked by dozens of channels.

Granite extraction and the manufacture of soda from kelp were for centuries Chausey's main trades, followed by shellfishing, which is still an important source of income, and tourism.

One of its largest attractions is its wildlife, particularly sea birds, and flora, which thrives in the microclimate.

Chausey, a listed site where building and hunting are prohibited, is jointly owned and maintained by the French Coastal Protection Agency (*Conservatoire du Littoral*), the town of Granville and the Chausey Islands Real Estate Company. It was included under the scope of Natura 2000.

Below

The Sound, a narrow stretch of sea, separates Grande Ile, on the right on the photo, from the small islands at the east of the archipelago.

VILLEDIEU-LES-POÊLES

Returning from chausey, head for Villedieu-les-Poêles. This typical Norman town, which has been awarded the status *Ville et métiers d'art* (traditional arts and crafts town), became an important centre for the copperware industry in the 12th century. This industry was established in the town by the Knights of Malta, who still don their ceremonial dress every four years to take part in the *Grand Sacre* procession. The *Atelier du Cuivre* (Copper Workshop) keeps both the production and techniques of this industry alive, and in the nearby *Musée de la Poêlerie – Maison de la Dentellière* visitors can discover the history and the art of copperware and lace-making. Villedieu also has a tin museum. However, the town is known mostly today as the home of one of the last bell foundries in France, Cornillé-Havard. Both the secular and ultra-modern processes used to cast bells are open to the public and are always very popular. On the road to Coutances, in Gavray, the Dukes of Normandy built a vast fortress on top of the hill overlooking the river Sienne; its remains have been partially restored and opened to the public.

In the Sienne valley stands the Abbey of Hambye, with its romantic ruined belltower and nave. The monastery's chapter house, sacristy, mortuary, calefactory and agricultural premises make up some of the finest monastic buildings in Normandy. The lay monks' building now hosts the *Conservatoire de la Manche*, with its collection of liturgical clothing and objects. In the neighbouring town of Savigny, the fine Romanesque Church of Notre-Dame is decorated with numerous original modillions and attractive frescos.

Above, right
The bell with the inscription marking its blessing.

Above, left
Casting metal at the bell foundry in Villedieu-les-Poêles. The molten metal has been heated to 1,200 degrees.

COUTANCES

Coutances, sub-prefecture of the Manche, is an episcopal town with a long history, today renowned for its popular jazz festival *Sous les Pommiers*. There are some remains of an aqueduct, which used to supply the town of *Cosedia*, later known as *Constantia*. The pride of the town is the cathedral, with its 77-metre high twin spires and remarkable lantern tower, *le Plomb*. With its delicate, graceful columns and vaults and beautiful mediaeval stained-glass windows, Coutances cathedral is considered the finest example of Norman Gothic art. It was built in the 13th century on the site of a Roman sanctuary by the sons of Tancrède de Hauteville, Lord of Hauteville-la-Guichard, who founded the kingdom of Pouilles and Sicily in the 12th century, as recalled in a commemorative plaque in the church and a small museum in this, their home town. The Churches of Saint-Pierre and Saint-Nicolas are fine examples of Renaissance or late Gothic architecture. The lantern tower which rises above the Church of Saint-Pierre represents a tiara; Pope Alexander VI contributed to its construction.

The *Jardin des plantes* (botanical gardens) in Coutances was one of the first parks in France to be listed.

If you visit the Château of Gratot in the surrounding area, you will hear of the legend of the Fairy Tower. At the Château of Pirou, you will learn of the legend of the geese of Pirou. Inside this castle, a tapestry also evokes the conquest of Italy by the Guiscard de Hauteville family. In Canville-la-Roque, a fresco in the church tells the story of the Miracle of the Hanged Innocent.

Top, left
Turning themselves into geese to escape their assailants, the defenders of the Château of Pirou were never again to regain their human form because the necessary magic spell was lost forever.

Top, right
On the horizon, the twin spires of Coutances cathedral. In the background is the lantern tower of Saint-Pierre, a fine Renaissance building.

Right page
The chevet on the lantern tower of Coutances cathedral, which exudes spirituality both inside and out.

LESSAY

Between Le Havre de Saint-Germain and a heath made famous in Barbey d'Aurevilly's novel *L'Ensorcelée*, the village of Lessay grew up around an abbey founded in the 11th century by Eudes au Capel. Destroyed during the war and rebuilt stone by stone, the abbey church is a masterpiece of Romanesque art, which strikes a perfect balance between its central square tower, apse and nave. Inside, lit by modern stained-glass windows inspired by Irish manuscripts, the sober décor of high altar, baptistry and liturgical furniture give the church a strong feeling of peace. In the autumn, Lessay hosts the Holy Cross Fair, which attracts over 100,000 visitors.

Neighbouring Mont Castre is reputed to be the site where Sabinus defeated the Unelli led by Viridovix as related by Julius Caesar in the *Gallic Wars*. However, some historians dispute this. Nevertheless, there are fabulous views, and sometimes you can see as far as the coast of England.

Above

Destroyed during the war, Lessay abbey church, founded in 1056 and dedicated to the Holy Trinity, was rebuilt stone by stone. It is a treasure of Romanesque art.

Valognes

The spirit of Barbey d'Aurevilly, the "Constable of Literature", haunts the towns of Saint-Sauveur-le-Vicomte and Valognes. The great writer was buried in the graveyard under the shadow of the high fortress of Saint-Sauveur. His manuscripts, notes and clothes are on display in his childhood home at the end of the Grand-Rue.

A favourite meeting-place among the nobility, the neighbouring town of Valognes became known as the "Versailles of Normandy". Despite the ravages of war, it has retained a good number of mansions, whose majestic façades line the streets or are tucked away in parkland. The finest examples include the *Hôtel de Beaumont*, the *Hôtel de Thieuville*, the *Hôtel de Granval-Caligny* (where Barbey d'Aurevilly lived for a time) and the *Maison du Grand Quartier*. Some of these historical monuments are now museums (celebrating cider, brandy and ancient trades and crafts) and are open to the public.

Left
The *Hôtel de Beaumont*, one of the finest mansions in Valognes, the "Versailles of Normandy".

Below
The fortress of the Neels and d'Harcourts, famous Norman barons in Saint-Sauveur-le-Vicomte, where Barbey d'Aurevilly was born on 2 November 1808.

Below
These bare-branched tamarisk trees are evidence of the violence of the winds that blow in from the narrow channel of *Raz Blanchard*, here in Goury, the famous sea rescue station and a village caught between land and sea.

LA HAGUE

You can get to La Hague via Barneville-Carteret or Bricquebec. From the *Cap de Carteret*, there is a remarkable view over Jersey, Guernsey, Alderney and Sark, "pieces of the kingdom of France", which fell into the hands of the English crown and which jealously guard their statutes and particularities.

The harbour of Carteret, on the Gerfleur, and that of its sister town, Portbail – whose Church of Notre-Dame on the banks of the harbour boasts the only known Gallo-Roman baptistery north of the Loire – are the main departure points from the Cotentin to the Channel Islands. Bricquebec, a mediaeval stronghold

which still has its castle and parapet walk linking the keep to the clock-tower, offers a pleasant walk.

Discover the peninsula of La Hague on a day when the Noroît, the famous north-west wind, chases the last clouds away. It is at times like these that the landscape really stands out and shows its character.

The moors and prairies, divided into an intricate patchwork by low stone walls to shelter them from the wind, are reminiscent of Brittany or Ireland. So are its hamlets, with their low houses with thick granite or schist walls. And so is its coastline, a succession of promontories and deep coves: Flamanville, Jobourg, Voidries, La Hague, Sciotot, Vauville, Ecalgrain. In Goury, a few cable lengths away from a famous sea rescue station, the lighthouse of *Gros du Raz* stands firm against the foaming currents of *Raz Blanchard*, which are the most feared and violent in Europe. Beyond La Hague, Port Racine, the smallest port in France, offers shelter to a handful of boats.

Right
The keep of the Château of Bricquebec.

Below
In Omonville-la-Petite, the inside of Jacques Prévert's house.

Climb up to the *Calvaire des Dunes* in Biville, a place of pilgrimage, and view the landscape in all its glory…

On the peninsula, you will also discover the burial mound of the Hougue Bie, which attests to a very early human presence on this site. The château and park of Flamanville and the botanical gardens at Vauville, where a microclimate allows exotic plants to grow, are also worth a visit. Visit Omonville-la-Petite and the home of poet Jacques Prévert and, in the *Vallée des Moulins* in Saint-Germain-des-Vaux, the garden which his wife, together with other artists, created in his memory. In Gréville-Hague, visit the birthplace of artist Jean-François Millet, the chronicler of peasant life. In Omonville-la-Rogue, visit the *Manoir de Tourp* and the *Maison de la Hague*. In Urville-Nacqueville, visit the *Manoir de l'Ecu* and English park, one of the finest on the Cotentin peninsula, and in Bricquebosq, visit a 15th-century fortified manor house, the *Grande Maison* (Great House).

Don't miss the Chapel of Saint-Germain in Querqueville, one of the oldest sanctuaries in France. Next, have a look at Cherbourg harbour, which offers constantly changing views. Before leaving the town, the *Fort du Roule* to the east of the town offers a different but equally remarkable panoramic view.

The Flamanville power station, home to the soon-to-be opened pressurised water reactor EPR, and ANDRA, a radioactive waste storage centre, make La Hague a hub of the nuclear industry. In Beaumont-Hague, the AREVA NC COGEMA plant provides information on these centres for the general public. AREVA even offers a free circuit across La Hague to show the measures that have been taken to protect the peninsula's environment.

Right page
The bay of Ecalgrain on the La Hague peninsula, one of its most beautiful locations.

Below
"The Cotentin … this rich, bustling land has, like its neighbour Brittany… its barren areas." Barbey d'Aurevilly, *L'Ensorcelée*. Below, the dunes at Biville.

CHERBOURG-OCTEVILLE

Cherbourg owes its existence to its geographical position and... to England, the "secular enemy" against which the statue of Napoleon raises its arm.

Although Maréchal Vauban in the 17th century first imagined the role that Cherbourg could play, located as it is in a deep bay, mid-way between the formidable capes of Barfleur and La Hague, at the point where the Channel meets the Atlantic, work on the harbour did not start until 1776. The *Grande Digue*, or Great Dyke, designed by La Bretonnière, surmounted by three forts, is an astonishing feat. It bars access to Querqueville harbour from Île Pelée. The other dykes, *Digue du Homet* and *Digue des Hollandais*, lengthen the harbour. All these works, military and civilian ports, were inaugurated by Napoleon III in 1858.

History proved these dykes to be futile. In an ironic twist of fate, in August 1944, after it was liberated by the Americans, it was English troops which cleared the port of mines laid by the Germans, enabling it to be used for supplying Allied troops until the armistice. The naval dockyard, which extends at length to the west of the town, is nowadays Cherbourg's contribution to national defence. It mostly designs and builds submarines.

A former stopover for Atlantic liners, Cherbourg has suffered from the transfer of passenger numbers from sea to air. Only ferries from England and Ireland now call to port. Cherbourg has made a vast science and culture centre from the constructions dating from this time. The *Grande Halle*, the Great Hall where trains dropped off passengers heading for America from all over Europe, the marine terminal itself, a fine example of 1930s Art Deco, have been renovated and new buildings added to create the *Cité de la Mer* museum. The abyssal aquarium, the deepest in Europe, houses in its 350,000 litres of water thousands of tropical and deep sea fish; the tactile pool enables visitors to touch some species. The Submarine Gallery recalls the period of the *Nautilus* and also reveals the entire history of the conquest of the ocean depths, of which Henri Germain Delauze was the pioneer, with displays of the instruments used. The vast entrance hall also houses the famous bathyscaphe, *Archimède*. One of the highlights of the *Cité de la Mer* is a visit, with audio guide, of the now disarmed nuclear submarine *Le Redoutable*.

The town of Cherbourg was built away from the quays and docks. It is a pleasant town, far removed from the image portrayed in films, literature and weather bulletins. The cloisters, church and monastic buildings of the Abbey of Notre-Dame-du-Voeu, the mediaeval Church of Saint-Martin with its sundial, the Emmanuel-Liais museum and park, the Montebello garden, the public garden, the altarpiece of the Church of the Trinité, the Thomas-Henry museum with its rich collection of works by Fra Angelico, Camille Claudel and Jean-François Millet, the Emmanuel-Liais museum and the botanical gardens make up its artistic heritage. The parks and Châteaux of Martinvast and Tourlaville, a magnificent house of blue granite built during the Renaissance and marked by the tragic memory of the Ravalet family, are also worth a visit when in Cherbourg.

Above

A fresco on the pediment of the *Cité de la Mer* in Cherbourg evokes the glorious bygone era of transatlantic voyages, sailing from the "inn of the Channel", as Maréchal Vauban put it.

BARFLEUR, SAINT-VAAST

From Cherbourg, a network of routes lead to the east coast of Cotentin via the valley of Saire, a friendly region which was home to Alexis de Tocqueville, the 18th-century historian and philosopher and a good lord to his people.

The Gatteville lighthouse offers an unequalled vantage point over the *Raz de Barfleur* – as long as you climb the 365 steps to the summit. Barfleur, where sea spray sometimes hits the belltower, holds the memory of a distant tragedy. The *Blanche Nef* set sail from here in 1120, bringing the court and children of Henry I to England. Only a baker survived to tell the tale of the shipwreck. According to the chronicles of the time, the king never smiled again.

In 1692, the bay enclosed by the *Pointe de Saire* headland was the scene of one of the French navy's worst disasters in history. After trying in vain to pass *Raz Blanchard*, thirteen ships of Admiral Tourville's fleet came here to shelter and ran aground. All the English had to do was set them on fire. In the bay of Saint-Vaast-la-Hougue, the small island of Tatihou, which has been put to many uses over the centuries, is now a highly popular tourist destination. The fortress and Vauban Tower and the maritime garden there are well worth a visit.

Linked to the sea by a canal, Carentan is the starting point for walks and excursions in the regional park of the *Marais du Cotentin et du Bessin*, with its museum at Marchésieux. From the *Ponts d'Ouve* in Saint-Côme-du-Mont, visitors can follow the Douve, the Orne, the Vire and other rivers that irrigate the vast Central Manche area, a land of nature, tradition and ancient crafts. The beach which extends from the dunes of Varéville to the *baie des Veys*,

Below

The Barfleur fishing fleet waits for the tide. In the background, the church, which is practically a fortress, dates from the 17th century.

which can be discovered at the museum in the *Manoir de Cantepie*, is none other than Utah Beach, where the Americans mounted their assault on Sainte-Marie-du-Mont on the morning of 6 June 1944, setting up a link with Sainte-Mère-Eglise where troops had parachuted during the night. A dummy paratrooper hangs from the belltower of Sainte-Mère, recalling an episode in this assault, which is also depicted on the church's stained-glass windows.

Above
The 71-metre-high lighthouse of Gatteville is the second-tallest in France.

Right
The towers of Notre-Dame in Saint-Lô ruined by the bombings were left untouched during rebuilding work.

Below
A paratrooper of the 82nd Airborne Division landed on the belltower of Sainte-Mère-Eglise and remained there for many hours. This is the episode recalled by the dummy.

SAINT-LÔ

"The capital of ruins" in 1944, Saint-Lô, prefecture of the Manche – called Briovère until the 11th century – was rebuilt by its inhabitants.

On the summit of a shale escarpment overlooking the Vire valley, the ramparts and towers around the walls attest to its history: Saint-Lô was a stronghold, and was often besieged, invaded, pillaged and even laid waste. But since the devastation of 1944, nothing remains of the town, which prospered in the shelter of the stronghold, and where weavers, cutlers, tanners and goldsmiths once made it the third largest Normandy town before fleeing after the Edict of Nantes. Notre-Dame, illuminated by mediaeval and contemporary stained-glass windows, retained only the two heavily damaged towers of a façade which so enchanted Victor Hugo. Modern buildings housing the prefecture and administrative offices have replaced the picturesque buildings of yesteryear. Located outside the town walls, the Romanesque Church of Sainte-Croix was the site of one of the most famous episodes in the battle of Saint-Lô, involving Major Howie.

The *Musée du Bocage Normand* (Museum of Normandy Countryside) at Bois-Jugan farm and statue of the *Laitière normande* celebrate Saint-Lô's role as capital of a dairy region. The stud farm is also popular with visitors. Set up by Napoleon, located in 19th-century Renaissance-style buildings and restored in 1945, it houses some sixty stallions of various races, specialising in the French saddle horse. It is one of the largest stud farms in France.

Rebuilt somewhat contentiously, the *Musée des Beaux Arts* – the Jean-Lurçat arts centre – gives pride of place to two treasures: a stele, known as the Thorigny Marble, discovered in 1580 in Vieux-la-Romaine, in the neighbouring *département*, and the famous tapestries of Flanders illustrating the life of Gombault and Macé.

The Chapel of La Madeleine, formerly a leprosarium, is now a US memorial.

There are many châteaux in the surrounding area, where the *Roches de Ham* offer a spectacular view over the Vire valley. The most famous is Torigny-sur-Vire, the former residence of the Matignon family. The Château de Canisy, a stunning architectural ensemble set in lush greenery, has been turned into an internationally-renowned culture centre by the descendents of the family who have owned the castle since the Middle Ages.

CERISY-LA-FORÊT

Founded in 1032 on the remains of a monastery by Robert the Magnificent, who dedicated it to Saint Vigor, the Abbey of Cerisy-la-Forêt is the centrepiece of Romanesque art in Normandy.

Although it lost several of its nave bays in the 19th century, the church remains a magnificent work of art, in particular for its apse which boasts three-storey-high windows. Large-scale restoration work was undertaken and a lapidary museum was opened in the monastic buildings, which include a courtroom, abbey chapel and archive room. The Abbey of Cerisy today provides an attractive backdrop to the conferences and cultural events held here.

Leave the Manche on a green – or religious – note: explore the park with eight lakes at Saint-Germain-d'Elle, where the river of the same name has its source. Or visit Trois-gots, where La Chapelle-sur-Vire has been a pilgrimage destination since the 12th century.

Below
Extensive ramparts protected the old town of Saint-Lô.

Below
A Romanesque masterpiece, the Abbey of Saint-Vigor in Cerisy-la-Forêt stands in a superb setting.

LA ROCHE BLEUE

Calvados

The Constituent Assembly of the French Revolution chose to name this area the *département* of Calvados, after the *Salvador*, a Spanish ship, which was shipwrecked off the coast. It therefore has nothing to do with the famous drink, despite producing it in large quantities.

Left page
In Honfleur, the high façades, protected by shingles, on Saint-Catherine's quay, give the *Vieux Bassin* (old dock) a picturesque feel.

At 2,142 square miles, it is one of the smallest *départements* in Basse-Normandie but has the largest population: 650,000 inhabitants. It offers highly varied landscapes, including the hilly terrain and hedgerows of *Pays d'Auge* country, and the gorges of the Orne, not forgetting "Swiss Normandy", the beaches on the Côte Fleurie and the *Vaches Noires* cliffs.

Fringed with a low-lying 72-mile coastline, Calvados' highest point is Mont Pinçon, almost 365 metres high.

The reputation of its cream, butter, cheese, cider and calvados provides a measure of security to its farmers. After the closure of its iron and steel industries, the *département* turned to tertiary activities, of which tourism plays a major part.

Calvados is steeped in history, the first chapter of which was written by William the Conqueror, the most recent of which began on the morning of 6 June 1944.

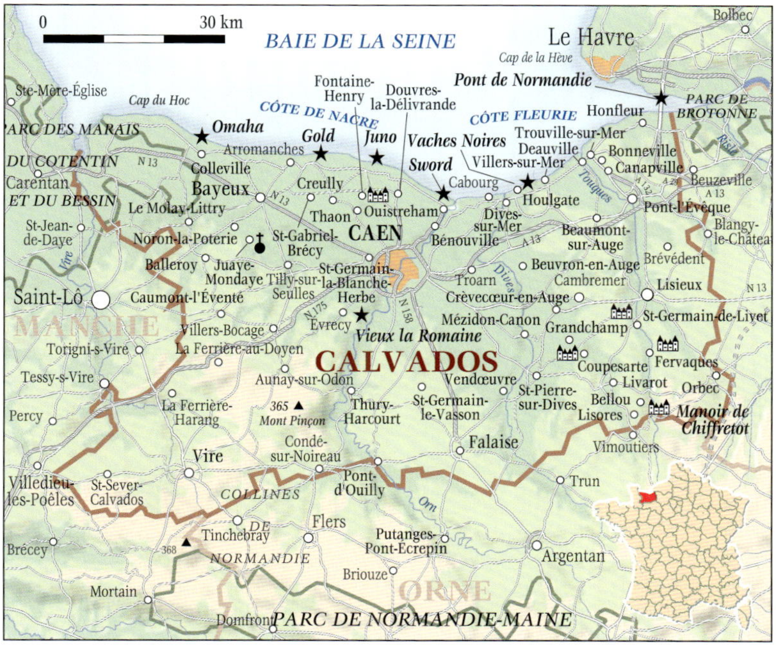

PAYS D'AUGE COUNTRY

The *pays d'Auge* country is, for many people, the image of Normandy. It is famous for its gastronomy and its *art de vivre*. Its cider and other cider-based products are to the *Pays d'Auge* what Bordeaux and Burgundy are to wine.

One of the best ways to discover it is via the south. Orbec, on the banks of the river Orbiquet, is typical of the area, with its church, Renaissance steeple and belltower surrounded by houses, mansions, an old manor house and the town museum, all half-timbered and pink-bricked.

Hidden in the valleys which lead to the sea lie manors and châteaux.

La Touques leads to Chiffretot, Bellou, Fervaques (where the ghost of the writer Châteaubriand roams) and Saint-Germain-de-Livet, with its chequered stone walls. North of the A13 motorway lie Canapville, with its *Manoir des Evêques* (bishops' manor), Ouilly-le-Vicomte, where the 16th-century Château de Boutemont is set in beautiful Classical- and Italian Renaissance-style grounds, and Bonneville, where William prepared to set sail for England. The river Vie will take you to Coupesarte, a beautiful wooden building, to Grandchamp, Mesnil-Mauger, Crèvecoeur-en-Auge, whose manor, headquarters of the

Below
Destroyed by fire in 1944, the covered market of Saint-Pierre-sur-Dives was rebuilt using materials and techniques from the 11th and 12th centuries.

Schlumberger foundation, has adorned so many books. Further west on the Dives lies Vendeuvre, with its water gardens and a rare museum of miniature furniture.

On these castle-lined roads, in Lisores, a fresco by Fernand Léger adorns the gable wall of the farm of La Bougonnière, a museum dedicated to the artist.

Right
Livarot cheeses during the manufacturing process. The five stripes banding the cheese have earned it the nickname "colonel".

Below
The small manor house of Crèvecoeur-en-Auge. Perhaps the most famous of all of Normandy's rustic-style houses.

In Livarot, the manufacture of famous Livarot cheese is a public event. Two towers, Romanesque and Gothic, indicate the Abbey of Saint-Pierre-sur-Dives. Its monastic buildings house a culture and information centre dedicated to cheese – the monks would be happy! But the true wonder of Dives is its covered market. Destroyed during the war, it was faithfully restored to its 13th-century glory: 300,000 chestnut pegs make up the enormous wooden framework which supports the roof.

Perched on a hill, Beaumont-en-Auge, the home town of the mathematician Laplace, provides a stunning view over the Touques valley. The neighbouring Beuvron-en-Auge equally has an outstanding view, this time over the Dives valley, from the Chapel of Clermont and the hundred-year-old beech grove which leads to it. Both villages have preservation orders and are the most typical villages of the *Pays Augeron*, if not of the whole of Basse-Normandie. With its timber-framed houses, inn, 18th-century presbytery and covered market (rebuilt in 1975 by the village's inhabitants themselves), Beuvron is even considered to be one of the most beautiful villages in all of France.

Badly damaged during the war, Pont-l'Evêque has preserved or restored some of its heritage, such as the *Hôtel de Brilly*, seat of the town hall and the former convent of the *Dames dominicaines de l'Isle*, the façade of which is decorated with a superb wooden gallery. The convent is now home to the Gustave-Flaubert arts centre. The writer often stayed at the Geffosses farm and based his tale *Un coeur simple* in Pont-l'Evêque. Foodlovers will recall that Pont-l'Evêque is also the name of one of the three great Normandy cheeses.

Left page
Beuvron-en-Auge, a village which is typical of this area right down to the detail of its façades.

Below
The vast dome of Sainte-Thérèse Basilica, in Lisieux, dominates the town itself and the Touques valley.

LISIEUX

Therese Martin, the daughter of a watchmaker-jeweller, came from Alençon to Lisieux, a sub-prefecture of Calvados and administrative capital of the *Pays d'Auge*, and turned it into a stronghold of Christianity and a destination for pilgrims worldwide.

The 100-metre high dome, nave and belltower of the basilica dedicated to St. Theresa of the Child Jesus stand tall and white on the slopes of the Touques valley, overlooking the town. The Romanesque Byzantine basilica, the work of architect Louis Marie Cordonnier and his sons and grandsons and decorated with marble and mosaics by Pierre Gaudin, was consecrated in 1954. It is without a doubt the largest 20th-century Christian sanctuary.

Before coming to pray to the author of *The Story of a Soul*, pilgrims can visit the places frequented by the saint during her lifetime, including *Les Buissonnets*, the family home she left at the age of fifteen to take holy orders, the Carmelite chapel, where a reliquary contains her relics, and the Church of Saint-Pierre, where she went to mass.

In a chapel of this church, built in the 12th and 13th centuries, lies Pierre Cauchon, bishop of Lisieux and chief judge in the trial of Joan of Arc. The former episcopal palace, one of the rare buildings to escape the fire which ravaged Lisieux in 1943, the Renaissance-style Church of Saint-Jacques, some timber-framed houses, one of which houses the Museum of Art and History, the remains of a Roman road which can be seen in the Médiathèque, the 18th-century mansions that house the town hall and the music school make up Lisieux's architectural heritage. The remains of a Roman road and of a Gallo-Roman town, and the archaeological garden are testimony to the long history of this town, where Eleanor of Aquitaine and Henry Plantagenet were married.

Above
The mosaics of Pierre Gaudin decorate most of the arches and walls of Saint-Thérèse Basilica.

HONFLEUR

Summer or winter, visitors flock to Honfleur to wander around the quays and the Saint-Léonard and L'Enclos districts, strolling down the picturesque streets of the largest listed area in France, or simply to "see the sea" at the end of the pier. Not many towns have so many tourist attractions and were spared during the war, as Honfleur was.

A stronghold for many years, Honfleur played a major part in the discovery of the world by sea. It was from here that Gonneville set out for Brazil and Samuel Champlain set out for Quebec. The people of Honfleur set up close links with the West Indies. They were some of the earliest to set out for Newfoundland. The shipyards here prospered for centuries and storehouses were built inside the Enclosure to store salt for preserving cod. Similarly, it was shipwrights who built the Church of

Below
The Vieux Bassin, or old dock, the heart of Honfleur.

Above
Today a famous hotel, Saint-Siméon farm-hostel, formerly owned by "the father and mother Toutain", was the favourite meeting-place of painters such as Boudin, Monet, Courbet and Jongkind.

Sainte-Catherine, giving its two naves the shape of an overturned hull. The museum of Vieux-Honfleur explores this past in great detail.

In the 19th century, artists such as Bonington, Turner and Isabey made the town famous.

Eugène Boudin, who was born here, befriended Courbet, Jongkind and Monet with whom he spent many happy hours at the farmhouse-inn Saint-Siméon.

Boudin was not a match for the great masters of his time but Camille Corot called him the "king of the skies" and Charles Baudelaire celebrated his ability to capture nuance. Quite rightly, the museum he helped to create is dedicated to him.

The trend launched over a hundred years ago has grown and grown. In present-day Honfleur, there are some eighty art galleries. Scarcely a day goes by without an artist setting up easel at the foot of La Lieutenance, the former residence of the governer on the banks of the Vieux-Bassin, where the slightest breeze ruffles the reflection of the tall houses on Saint-Catherine's quay.

Poets, musicians, historians and film-makers have also contributed to Honfleur's fame. Baudelaire adored this town. It was here that he wrote

The Albatross, *Man and the Sea* and *The Harbour*. History records the birth here of poet Henri de Régnier, historian Albert Sorel, the great Belle Epoque humorist Alphonse Allais and musician Erik Satie, whose birthplace "Les Maisons" is open to visitors.

Although the novels of Lucie Delarue-Mardrus are no longer widely read, her poems remain popular.

Honfleur's heritage includes the *pont de Normandie*, which locals call the "*pont de Honfleur*". Take a boat from the harbour to get the best view of this bridge, which stands almost 60 metres above the sea, spanning 2,141.25 metres, supported by two 215-metre pillars and 184 cables.

From Mont Joli and the Côte de Grâce, it has the allure more of a work of art than a feat of engineering.

At the summit of Côte de Grace, the Chapel of Notre-Dame-de-Grâce (built in the 17th century after the sanctuary constructed by Richard II fell into the sea) welcomes sea-faring pilgrims at Pentecost, come to implore the Virgin Mary. Their gratitude can be seen in the innumerable commemorative plaques and models hanging from the ceiling and marble-covered walls.

Below
The newest architectural masterpiece on the Seine estuary, the *pont de Normandie*, which locals call the "*pont de Honfleur*". At nightfall, the bridge can be admired from Côte Sainte-Catherine or Mont Joli.

THE CÔTE FLEURIE

From Villerville to Cabourg lies a chain of seaside resorts, populated each weekend by walkers and owners of holiday homes. Known as the twenty-first *arrondissement* of Paris, the Côte Fleurie is to Normandy what the Côte d'Azur is to Provence.

Seen from the coast road, Trouville and Deauville, situated on either bank of the Touques, seem to merge into one. They are distinct, however, each with its own sandy beach, boardwalk and casino.

Artists discovered Trouville in 1830, followed soon after by the first bathers. But the town grew around this fishing village without any proper planning, giving it its character and authenticity, but also some awkwardness. Trouville is a lively, animated, popular town. The quays of the colourful fishing port have been remarkably preserved and are well worth a visit. The *villa Montebello*, built by Marshal Lannes, now houses the arts centre. One room is dedicated to the history of sea bathing, while another commemorates novelist Marguerite Duras. Deauville was born some years later on the wasteland that was the left bank of the Touques on the initiative of the Duke of Morny, businessman and advisor to Napoleon III. Sensing where the future lay, he intended to create a seaside resort, a holiday town. The stained-glass windows of the Church of Saint-Augustin portray the laying of its foundation stone. The sea front, the large, flower-filled avenues, and the villas, such as the *villa Strassburger*, inspired by Augeron-style manor houses and cottages, make Deauville the town its founders dreamt of. Deauville is the place to be seen in Normandy and enjoys an international reputation. On the boardwalk near the *bar du Soleil*, the Pompei baths and the casino, the crowds indulge in some celebrity-spotting. There are three major events during the season: the racing in Clairefontaine and La Touques, the sale of yearlings, year-old foals from the

Left
The Church of Saint-Pierre, one of two sanctuaries in Touques, a small village on the river from which it takes its name.

Below
The rustic style of Normandy has provided much inspiration to the architects of Deauville's villas. The white stone, classical-style casino is one of the most popular in all of France.

most prestigious cross-breeds and the most famous stud farms, and the International American Film Festival. The temperature of the water in Deauville is not often the main subject of conversation.

Tired of the crowds? Go to Touques, climb Mont Canisy and visit Villers-sur-Mer. Large rocks have fallen from the cliff separating this resort from Houlgate. Covered in kelp, they look a little like a cowherd, hence their name. *Les Vaches Noires* (the Black Cows) is a listed site containing many fossils. Some fine specimens from here are on display at the Paleontology Museum of Villers.

Further west, another village on the Côte Fleurie, Cabourg, was also favoured by 19th-century bathers. The atmosphere here is a little less showy, a little more discreet.

The local cinema festival celebrates romance. Mansions and villas were built in a star pattern around the centre and casino, according to designs by the architect Robinet. In his "In the Shadow of Young Girls in Flower", Proust depicted the world of this resort, called Balbec in the novel.

From top to bottom

Hotel Normandy is typical of the architecture in Deauville.

The Casino Barrière in Deauville is one of the most popular casinos in France.

"*Les Planches*" in Deauville is a popular spot for fashionable resort life and can often be seen bustling with crowds.

He often stayed here – his lodging of choice was Room 414 in the Grand Hotel. On the beachfront promenade, named after him, you might meet the ghost of Albertine...

William the Bastard set sail from the Dives estuary in October 1066 for Hastings, where he would conquer Harold and be crowned King of England, becoming known as William the Conqueror. English families sometimes come to read the list of the 475 knights who accompanied him, inscribed on a plaque on the wall of the Church of Notre-Dame in Saint-Pierre-sur-Dives, in the hope of finding the name of their ancestor. The *Hostellerie Guillaume*, the covered market, the *Manoir du Bois Hibout* and the *Lieutenance* all bear witness to this town's history.

Above
The Church of Notre-Dame in Dives-sur-Mer was long known as the Church of Saint-Sauveur. Pilgrims used to come to see a statue of Christ, whose story is portrayed in a stained-glass window.

Right
The bedroom in the Grand Hotel where Marcel Proust used to stay in Cabourg.

Below
The seaside resort of Cabourg, known as "Balbec" in *In Search of Lost Time*, is completely built around the Grand Hotel.

THE CÔTE DE NACRE

On the morning of 6 june 1944, the beaches of the Côte de Nacre, between the estuaries of the Orne and the Vire, entered the history books, taking the name assigned to them on the Allies' maps: "Sword" lies between Ouistreham and Lion-sur-Mer, "Juno" between Bernières and Courseulles, "Gold" between Courseulles and Arromanches, and the bloody battlesite of "Omaha" between Vierville and Grandcamp. These beaches are now four stages on the Normandy Landings Tour. The other stages are in the Manche, where the Americans landed at Utah Beach, and on the banks of the river Orne, where Bénouville Bridge was famously taken on D-Day, during the night of 5-6 June 1944. This bridge, taken down and reconstructed and since known as Pegasus Bridge (Pegasus was the emblem of the British 6th Airborne Division which seized it), together with the replica of the *Horsa* glider on which the troops landed nearby, are exhibited in the Pegasus Memorial Museum in Ranville.

Thousands of people visit these historical sites every year. The sea and beaches have retained little physical evidence of this time. In Arromanches are the remains of the Mulberries, parts of the artificial port built by the Allies during the landings but which was destroyed by a storm a few days later. The land has retained deeper traces of the landings.

In Ouistreham, Colleville-Montgomery, Longues or the *Pointe du Hoc*, visit the pillboxes, bunkers and other fortifications along the Atlantic sea wall. Films and exhibitions in a dozen or so museums in the region tell the dramatic story of how English, Canadian and American troops took the coast.

Further inland, huge graveyards were built for the bodies of those who fell during this furious battle – in Colleville-Montgomery, Bayeux, Bény-sur-Mer and La Cambe.

Life still goes on in these pilgrimage destinations, however, with sites and monuments restored to their past glory. The sea draws people who want to get away from it all. The Château of Bénouville, designed by the architect Ledoux, the Château of Courseulles, a fortress which became a civil residence in the 16th and 17th centuries thanks to François d'O and later Anne Morat, the fortified church of Ouistreham, some villas in Lion-sur-Mer and the belltower of Bernières are the delight of amateurs of fine architecture. The basilica of Douvres-la-Délivrande is a destination for pilgrims worshipping the Black Virgin, as is the nearby chapel by René Lalique, built from glass tiles and dedicated to Notre-Dame de la Fidélité. The Château of Creully is a perfectly preserved mediaeval fortress which housed the BBC transmitter during the Battle of Normandy. The Château of Brécy looks out over a rare example of a 17th-century garden.

Left

The square keep of the Château of Creully, built in the 14th century.

Right
The fighting was so fierce on this beach on the morning of 6 June that Omaha Beach was nicknamed "Bloody Omaha".

Below
A short distance from Omaha, the graveyard of Colleville houses the graves of 9,386 American soldiers.

BAYEUX

Capital of Bessin, sub-prefecture of Calvados and a bishopric, Bayeux possesses an incomparable heritage that was spared the ravages of war.

Destroyed by fire in 891 by Rollo, Bayeux is the town where Harold swore an oath of allegiance to William the Conqueror, which he was later to break. Bayeux was the first town in France to be liberated, and Charles de Gaulle visited it a few days after the landing, making a famous speech here on 16 July 1946, which is considered the foundation of the Fifth Republic. A memorial recalls these two events. This town, steeped in history, honours those who record history today. Each year, it awards the Bayeux Calvados prize to war correspondents. The town also has a memorial dedicated to reporters.

The Cathedral of Notre-Dame is the most striking building in Bayeux. It has been rebuilt, modified and improved many times. The crypt and towers of the façade are the only remains of the sanctuary built by Bishop Odon, half-brother of William. The massive dome atop the central tower, known as "the Bonnet", is a 19th-century addition. The well-proportioned nave mixes Romanesque and Gothic styles, while the large arcades boast fine Norman Romanesque sculpture. The paintings decorating the vault of the Gothic choir depict the first bishops of Bayeux.

An old mill (Crocquevieille), an arch bridge, an old fish market and many mansions built between the 15th and 18th century, including *Hôtel d'Argouges*, *Maison du Cadran*,

Left page
The dome atop the lantern tower of the cathedral of Bayeux was not built until the 19th century. The towers of the façade date from the 11th century.

Below
Interesting 11th-century sculptures adorn the capitals of the crypt, which is also decorated with 15th-century frescoes.

Above
The mill wheel at Crocquevieille.

Hôtel de Rubery and *Hôtel Saint-Manvieux*, the public garden where a weeping beech has been officially recognised as a Remarkable Tree of France, and the banks of the river Aure all give this town great character. The *Hôtel du Doyen*, former residence of the dean of the cathedral chapter, houses the collections of the Baron-Gérard Museum (porcelain, paintings and lace). Nearby, in the *Conservatoire de la Dentelle*, a few talented lace-makers still weave using the Bayeux stitch.

The Bayeux tapestry is what has made the town famous. Perfectly restored and lit up in a room in the William the Conqueror centre, this tapestry, designed as a propaganda tool, tells the conquest of England in comic-book format, from beginning to end, and justifying the expedition. Made of wool embroidery on linen rather than an actual tapestry, 70 metres long and 50 centimetres high, it was commissioned by Odon in order to decorate the cathedral and believed to have been made in Kent, despite the legend attributing it to Queen Matilda. There are fifty-eight sequences – although some may have been lost – involving six hundred characters, making the Tale of the Conquest, as it is also known, an incomparable document on daily life, mores, crafts and techniques in the Middle Ages, as well as a description of the Battle of Hastings.

Nearby, in Le Molay-Littry, find out about the milling industry in the *Musée de la Meunerie*, housed in Marcy watermill, and discover the outstanding Périer brothers' fire machine, the most remarkable object in a museum devoted to the only coal mine ever opened in Normandy, which closed in 1949. The Château of Balleroy needs no introduction. Architect François Mansart, landscape gardener André Le Nôtre and artist Pierre Mignard made this castle a masterpiece. It was bought in 1970 by the American Malcolm Forbes, who created an extraordinary museum of hot air and gas balloons. The Châteaux of Audrieu and Condé-sur-Seulles, both built in the 18th century, the Château of Colombière, typical of the military architecture of the feudal era, the Château of Fontaine-Henry, with its vast roofs and outstanding sculpted façade, the Château of Vaulaville, built in the 'folly' style, and the Château of Brécy, with its stunning grounds, are some of Bessin's other delights. The church of the Abbey of Juaye-Mondaye is a rare example of classical religious architecture in Normandy. The village of Noron-la-Poterie is devoted to the manufacture of stoneware pottery.

In Caumont-l'Eventé, the "Souteroscope" opens the way to the underground slate quarries.

Left

Section 48 of the Bayeux Tapestry: William takes counsel from his half-brothers Odon, bishop of Bayeux, and Robert, Count of Mortain.

SWISS NORMANDY

Capital of the bocage country and sub-prefecture of Calvados, Vire is proud of its *andouille* or chitterling sausage; the songs of miller Olivier Basselin sung on the banks of the Vire were the precursor of "vaudeville".

Vire was badly damaged in the war, but has retained the remains of the stronghold it once was under Henry I Beauclerc. These remains include the keep, which overlooks the river. However, the most remarkable monument is the impressive clock-tower, flanked by two machicolated towers and topped with a belfry that is the gateway to the heart of the town.

Not far away, the Château of Pontecoulant, a model of harmony and sobriety, sold to the *département* of Calvados by the Pontecoulant family, is now a fine furniture museum.

From Putanges-Pont-Ecrepin in Orne to Thury-Harcourt in Calvados, the Orne, supplemented by the waters of the Noireau, has cut a deep bed. Its valley winds its way between rocks and forests, and is reminiscent of an Alpine valley.

A minister of the Third Republic called this place "Swiss Normandy". This delightful place must not be missed. The gorges of Saint-Aubert, the meandering Rovrou, the Cross of La Faverie and the *Pain de Sucre* (Sugar Loaf) will delight even the most demanding painters or photographers.

So will the fords of *Pont-d'Ouilly*, where the surprising Chapel of Saint-Roch is a major pilgrimage destination every August, Clécy, at the foot of *Rochers du Parc*, a favourite spot in Normandy for outdoor sports, and Saint-Rémi, whose church, with its Romanesque bell, stands in the shadow of a massive yew tree. The town's *Fosses d'Enfer* house the *Maison des Ressources Géologiques de Normandie*, which looks at 600 million years of geological formation in the area. Visitors will delight at the sight of nature perfectly regained where the Orne flows onto the plain in the grounds and garden of the Château of La Motte in Acqueville.

Left

The fortified gate of Vire is considered the finest in Normandy. The towers date from the 13th century, the belfry from the 15th century and the clock was installed in 1480.

Right page

Visitors will be surprised at the size and slope of the roofs of the pavilion adjoining the superb Château of Fontaine-Henry.

FALAISE

A statue by rochet of a rearing horse whose helmeted and armoured rider brandishes a spear is Falaise's homage to William the Conqueror, its native son.

He was born here in 1027, an illegitimate child, and sought refuge here several times when his enemies tried to assassinate him.

Legend and history often mingle here. In the Val d'Ante, at the foot of the fortress facing Mont Myrrha, a bas-relief shows the fountain where Arlette, the tanner's daughter, used to do her washing.

At the castle, you might see the window from which Robert saw and fell in love with her. She became his wife *more danico* and the mother of William. Whatever the truth in this story, Falaise was already a stronghold when William was born here in

Right

A statue of William on horseback by Rochet was unveiled in 1851 by the town of Falaise in honour of its most famous son.

Below

The Talbot tower, named after the man who built it, stands like a sentinel in front of the fortress of Falaise.

1027. But the 900 metres of ramparts encircling the old town, reinforced with twenty towers, were built after his rule. So were both the large and small keeps, built in 1123 by Henry I Beauclerc. The round Talbot tower flanks the square mass of the fortress to which it is linked by a curtain wall. Standing over 35 metres high, with walls as thick as 4 metres at the base, this tower, which bears the name of its architect, was commissioned by Philippe Auguste.

The churches of the Trinité, Saint-Laurent and Saint-Gervais had already been founded by the time William was born. The Church of Notre-Dame was built with a donation from Matilda, his wife. It is located in the district of Guibray, named after a horse market which drew people from all over France for nearly a thousand years, and which was already in existence at the time of the dukes. An important town during the Middle Ages, Falaise also played a part in the Battle of Normandy. A museum tells how the 7th German army was annihilated in the Falaise pocket. Nearby, the Church of Aubigny and its statues of the praying figures of the town's lords, and the Saint-Vigor Chapel in Saint-Martin-de-Mieux, where the Japanese artist Kuoji Takubo has successfully blended mediaeval and modern art, add to the religious heritage of the *Pays de Falaise* area.

Above
The Church of the Trinité in Falaise mixes Gothic and Renaissance styles.

Right
From the time of the dukes, many sanctuaries were built in Falaise. This is the Church of Saint-Gervais.

CAEN

Caen, prefecture of Calvados and of the Region of Basse-Normandie, is a metropolis where space is definitely not at a premium. The Orne and its tributary the Odon lie on a large plain where the city can extend at leisure. After being almost destroyed in 1944, Caen was sympathetically rebuilt. The white stone lightly tinged with ochre (*pierre de Caen*), for which Caen is famous, lends majesty, warmth and light to the buildings lining the roads of the city.

Caen is known as the Athens of Normandy. This is an allusion to its elegance and atmosphere but also to the role of the University of Caen, founded in 1432 by the Duke of Bedford, representative of the King of England who ruled over Normandy at that time. The university plays an important role in the life of the city, both because of its physical size – some 33 hectares – and its influence. On the university campus, the famous scale model of Ancient Rome by the architect Paul Bigot, officially classed as a *Monument Historique*, is admired by all fans of the Latin world and Roman history. A number of institutes and the Ganil cyclotron complex make it a centre for scientific research. Companies working in the quaternary sector have replaced the iron and steel industry, created in 1908 by Baron Thyssen. It closed down at the end of the last century after nearly one hundred years, with

Left page
The Church of Saint-Etienne in the *Abbaye aux Hommes*, Caen, was consecrated in 1077 by the Bishop of Avranches in the presence of William and his wife, Matilda.

Below
Caen, seen here from the gardens of the *Parc d'Ornano*, could also be called the "city of a hundred spires".

the loss of many jobs. Caen is an important port, with four large docks along the 7-mile canal that links it to the sea. Ouistreham, on the estuary, is the departure point for English-bound ferries.

Also known as the "Polyphonic city", Caen is first and foremost the city of William the Conqueror. Apart perhaps from Falaise, in no other Norman town is his presence and that of Matilda, his wife, still as tangible. This presence makes itself felt in the *Abbaye aux Hommes* and the *Abbaye aux Dames*, both built to appease the pope for William's marriage to his own cousin.

Left
The entrance of the Château of Caen. William oversaw the castle's early construction before it became the largest fortified enclosure in Europe.

Below
A monk of Bec and architect, Guillaume de la Tremblaye restored the monastic buildings of the *Abbaye aux Dames* and Abbaye aux Hommes in the 17th century. The former now houses Basse-Normandie regional council.

William died in Rouen and was buried in Saint-Etienne, the church in the *Abbaye aux Hommes*. A slab in the chancel covers his tomb, which was desecrated several times. Only a single femur of the sovereign remains. Better to imagine him attending the consecration of the sanctuary in 1077.

Although often redesigned, the Church of Saint-Etienne has maintained its integrity, harmoniously combining Romanesque and Gothic styles. The handsome façade, flanked by two towers surmounted by the twin spires that often symbolise Caen, was built during his reign.

The adjoining monastic buildings of Saint-Etienne are the work of Guillaume de La Tremblaye. They used to house the Lycée François-Malherbe, named after the Caen-born poet who set the rules of French classicism. Today, they house the city hall. The grand staircase, guards' hall, tapestries and panelling in the refectory and the chapter room are much admired.

The *Abbaye aux Dames* looks out over the lake of Saint-Pierre. Squat, massive and deprived of its spires since the 18th century, the Church of the Trinité is neither as big nor as bold as Saint-Etienne. Its beauty lies in its sobriety, particularly that of the nave, which is in pure Romanesque style. Sixteen columns support the vault of a particularly remarkable crypt. In the chancel, a black marble slab commemorates Queen Matilda, who was buried here.

The abbey buildings – main courtyard, cloisters, lavabo and vestibule – were restored in the 17th century by Guillaume de La Tremblaye and were saved from destruction by the Basse-Normandie regional council, which set up headquarters here.

But it is doubtless the château, located in the city centre and extended by the Esplanade de la Liberté, which really makes Caen William's city. It was damaged during the war and restored, and is still undergoing restoration work which aims to make

Above

The entrance to the château in Caen, whose foundation stone was laid by William, and which became the largest fortified enclosure in Europe over the course of the centuries.

Below

The 78-metre high belltower of Saint-Pierre in Caen, "king of the Norman belltowers".

this important site of Anglo-Norman history a major tourist destination. Its enormous ramparts, standing clear and shown perfectly to advantage, rise up above the marina bordering the city centre. Although construction was started under the duke in 1060, the fortress, which is accessed via a gate heavily fortified with a barbican, probably owes no more than its location and footprint to him.

William's son Henry I Beauclerc reinforced it with a keep, which was destroyed during the National Convention, but work to render it impregnable continued until the 15th century. Thirteen towers reinforce the walls surrounding the largest fortified enclosure in Europe. This particularly mediaeval site, which even boasts a carefully-tended medicinal garden, houses the *Salle de l'Echiquier* – the formal room of the Normandy Court –, the Chapel of Saint-Georges, formerly a parish church, and the governor's residence, now home to the Normandy museum. The Fine Arts museum, with its remarkable collection of 16th- and 17th-century paintings, is also housed here, together with an open-air sculpture park with works by Bourdelle, Rodin, Giacometti, Cabanes and Huang Yong Ping. From the ramparts, the view extends as far as the sea and provides a wonderful glimpse of Caen itself, which seems to deserve the title given to Rouen by Victor Hugo, that of the "city of a hundred spires".

The neighbouring Church of Saint-Pierre is a masterpiece of Flamboyant art. Its 78-metre belltower, which was destroyed during the war, holds the disputed title of "king of the Norman belltowers". The vaults of the chancel, the chevet and the ambulatory chapels are richly decorated. Another wonder of Flamboyant art is Saint-Jean, whose impressive lantern tower rises from the transept. If you look closely, you will notice a slight tilt, which can also been seen from the nave. The instability of the ground on which the church is built means that the spire and pinnacles, which would have made it a replica of Saint-Pierre, could not be added.

The Church of Notre-Dame de Froide Rue has two naves. The remaining sanctuaries in Caen, some of which have fallen into disuse, are representative of many different styles and include the churches of Saint-Sauveur, Saint-Nicolas, Saint-Laurent, Notre-Dame-de-la-Gloriette and Saint-Michel-de-Vaucelles. Surviving examples of civil architecture are more rare, but noteworthy buildings include the *Hôtel d'Escoville*, the *Mai-*

Below, right
The Museum of Fine Art in Caen, inside the château ramparts. Refurbished in 1994, it houses remarkable collections from 16th- and 17th-century Italian, Flemish, Dutch and French masters.

Below, left
The *Esplanade du Mémorial* in Caen.

son des Quatrans, one of Caen's rare half-timbered buildings which houses the Post and Telecommunications Museum, the *Hôtel de Thaon*, the *Hôtel de Colomby* with its severe appearance, and the pleasure pavilion of the *Hôtel de Mondrainville*.

Any visit to Caen, which devotes an entire museum to nature near its city hall, should include some of its many green spaces, such as the Prairie, which provides the city with some welcome breathing space; the *Esplanade de l'hôtel de ville*, a real Norman garden; the highly original Luna-Rossa garden, which combines floral art and sculpture; the botanical garden, which boasts some 8,000 species of plants; the arboretum of the *Vallée des Jardins*; the *Parc Michel-d'Ornano*; the *Parc Saint-Paul* and the floral park of the 17-hectare *Colline aux Oiseaux*, which contains 570 varieties of roses.

The Memorial on the outskirts of the city confirms Caen's desire to become a place for reflecting on recent world history and peace. The two wings of this white-stone building on the *esplanade Eisenhower* have no windows in the façade and are separated by a small "breach". This breach symbolises the opening made by the last world war in the history of the world. Although part of its col-

Above

Not far from the village of Thaon, hidden in a lush, green valley, this little church – long in disuse – is a masterpiece of Romanesque art.

Right

The Chapel of Saint-Georges in the enclosure of the Château of Caen, formerly a parish church.

lections and exhibitions are devoted to the Battle of Normandy, the Memorial is not simply another WWII museum. Rather, it attempts to explore the origins and consequences of the conflict. Five hours should be set aside for a visit. Many conferences and conventions have taken place here, making Caen a centre for reflection and exchange to promote peace.

History has left its mark on the surrounding area. Two thousand years ago, the city of *Aregenua* lay on the outskirts of Caen. This capital of the Viducasses tribe is now the town of Vieux-la-Romaine. A museum, a large house which has been partially reconstructed, and an antique garden displaying the excavation work carried out on this site from 1703 to the present day help visitors to learn about daily life in a Gallo-Roman city. The more adventurous can even enjoy a Roman meal!

Other treasures include the Church of Saint-Pierre in Thaon, dating from the 11th and 12th centuries, the Abbey of Ardenne in Saint-Germain-la-Blanche-Herbe, and the 18th-century Château of Canon. This impressively-proportioned Italianate residence was built by Elie de Beaumont, the lawyer responsible for rehabilitating Jean Calas. Elie de Beaumont took extreme care with the garden and park, using both English and French landscaping techniques. Statues and follies abound in these wonderfully restored grounds, with lakes, waterfalls and streams, while flowers and fruit mature in the shelter of the charterhouses. The *Carreau de Livet* in Saint-Germain-le-Vasson brings to life the region's last iron mine, Soumont, as if it were yesterday.

Above
The façade of the Château de Canon, built by Elie de Beaumont for his wife, is reflected in one of the lakes in the grounds.

Above right
Protected from the wind by high walls, flowers bloom and fruit ripens quickly in one of the thirteen "charterhouses" in the gardens of the Château of Canon.

Opposite
Rich in the symbolism which was fashionable in the 18th century, follies and statues abound in the castle grounds.

Orne

The Orne is the only *département* in Normandy with no coastline. The air here is scented only with the aroma of farmland, which is just as pungent and revitalising as that of iodine. The air here is bracing too, with the *Signal* in the forest of Ecouves the highest point in Normandy at 417 metres.

Left page
Surrounded by the graveyard, above a field of rape in flower, the rustic Church of Sérans is like a symbol of the eternal renewal of life.

Its best-known areas are Perche and Passais. The forest, which has some particularly fine specimen trees, is one of the Orne's major attractions. It extends over 103,000 hectares in a territory of over 2,300 square miles. The best time to visit the Orne is in the spring and autumn.

This most discreet and rural of the *départements* of Normandy, with its small population (293,000 inhabitants) and no large town, is as captivating as its neighbours and a favourite among nature-lovers. The regional nature park of Le Perche, created in 1998, extends 180,000 hectares to the east while the regional nature park of Normandie-Maine, created in 1975, covers 235,000 hectares and is shared with the *départements* of Manche, Mayenne and Sarthe. The meadows are just as beautiful as the woodland. The workhorses and trotting horses that graze here are the pride of the Orne. Lace is another, quite different, longstanding tradition in Alençon and Argentan.

The region has as many châteaux as in the rest of Normandy, some of which are among the region's finest. The Abbey of Soligny, with its vow of silence, is as famous as other monasteries. Several pages of history have been written here since the Middle Ages. In Domfront and Tinchebray, history goes back several centuries; in Chambois, where the Battle of Normandy ended, it is more recent.

D'OUCHE-EN-PERCHE

In Saint-Evroult-Notre-Dame-du-Bois is the Abbey of Saint-Evroult, where Orderic Vital wrote his *Ecclesiastical History*, depicting Normandy

Left

The ruins of the Abbey of Saint-Evroult-Notre-Dame-du-Bois, founded in the 6th century, where Orderic Vital, who lived here from the age of 10 and died here, wrote his monumental *Ecclesiastical History.*

Below

The church and convent buildings of the Trappist Abbey of Soligny, where the religious community lives in total isolation and silence.

in a favourable light. The abbey is now a ruin on the border between the Eure and the Orne in a charming setting of water and greenery. In L'Aigle, the Flamboyant tower of the Church of Saint-Martin has a more austere appearance, being built with a stone typical of the *Pays d'Ouche* country, *grison*. Low in iron content, this stone gave rise to the metallurgy trade in the region, as related in the museum of the Grosse-Forge in Aube. Still in Aube, you can visit the Château des Nouettes, where the Countess of Ségur, author of *Pauvre Blaise, Les Malheurs de Sophie* and *Général Dourakine* among others, once lived.

In Soligny a community of Trappist monks lives in absolute silence and isolation. The abbey, founded in 1140 by the Benedictines in a setting of deep woods dotted with ponds, is not open to visitors but there is a video available on its history. Châteaubriand recounted the story of its most famous abbot, Rancé, who retired here after a turbulent life and reformed the Cistercian Order, introducing the rule of Strict Observance.

Right
The tower of the Church of Saint-Martin in L'Aigle, which means "The Eagle", so called, according to 19th-century writer La Varende, after an enormous nest was found in its forest.

MORTAGNE-AU-PERCHE

The last territory to be conquered by the Dukes of Normandy, Perche owes its fame to the stocky Percheron horse and to its hills. In Mortagne-au-Perche, you can visit the birthplace of the philosopher and moralist Alain, author of *Propos d'un Normand* (Tales of a Norman) and the austere *Maison des comtes du Perche*. The artistic heritage of this small, modest town, whose black pudding alone makes it worth a visit, includes some fine 18th-century houses, the cloisters of the convent of Saint-François, the crypt of Saint-André, the pews and altar in the Church of Notre-Dame and a number of sundials. A stained-glass window in the Church of Notre-Dame recalls the large part played by the town's inhabitants in the founding of Quebec. In the nearby small town of Tourouvre, the *Maison de l'Emigration française au Canada* tells the story of the French settlers in Canada.

Left

A stone's throw from the *Maison des comtes du Perche* stands the statue of the moralist and philosopher Alain, whose real name was Emile Chartier (1868-1951).

Below

Perched on a hilltop, the small town of Mortagne-au-Perche, on the border of Normandy. Alain, its most famous inhabitant, argued that Perche was truly Norman.

BELLÊME

To the south of Perche lies Bellême, land of fables, which appears to rise up over the river Huisne. The gate and towers are those of a town that has been besieged many times, notably by Blanche of Castile and the future Saint Louis. Its finest houses, located on the *rue de la Ville-Close*, date from the 17th and 18th centuries. The classical-style Church of Saint-Sauveur holds many treasures originally from neighbouring abbeys, including the canopied altar, stained-glass windows and panelling in the chancel, which all come from the Abbey of Valdieu. Every September, Bellême hosts the International Mycology Festival, attracting specialists from all over the world. Between conferences, they carry out their research in the beautiful nearby forests, beech and oak woods and mysterious ponds in Reno-Valdieu – next to which stands the neo-Gothic basilica of Notre-Dame-de-Montligeon, where pilgrims come from all over the world to pray for the dead –, Bellême and, further afield, Longny. In Nocé, Courboyer, one of Perche's many manor houses, houses the headquarters of the Perche regional nature park. The Saint-Cyr-la-Rosière rural museum, in the shadow of the magnificent Priory of Sainte-Gauburge, describes developments from the 19th century to the present day.

Above

The manor house of Courboyer, built in the 15th century, houses the headquarters of the Perche regional nature park.

ALENÇON

Alençon, prefecture town of the Orne, is not the only town where lace, so indispensable in former times, was produced, but it has acquired a worldwide reputation for it. The needlepoint stitch invented by Madame de La Perrière won the recognition of her contemporaries. Jean-Baptiste Colbert founded the Alençon lace workshops in 1665 to block imports from Venice and Flanders, thus contributing to the town's wealth. The Museum of Fine Arts and Lace-Making housed in the former Jesuit college offer you the opportunity to appreciate the intricacy and delicacy of this art. In contrast to other towns, Alençon's architectural heritage is dispersed over several different districts. In the town centre, you can tour a massive rotunda with an imposing slate-roof topped with a metal and glass dome. This is the 19th-century wheat market. Today it houses the arts centre. In the renovated district of Saint-Léonard, some mediaeval houses are reflected in the waters of the Sarthe. Further west, four towers, including the *Tour Couronnée*, give an idea of the dimensions of the château built by Jean Le Beau and the Dukes of Alençon. This château has now largely disappeared and its fortress has become a prison. A few fine mansions, some of which were immortalised by Honoré de Balzac in his novels *An Old Maid* and *The Collection of Antiquities*, are now administrative offices: the town hall occupies the former summer palace, the *Hôtel de Guise*, formerly home to the tax inspectorate, houses the prefecture and the tourist information centre is housed in the *Hôtel d'Ozé*.

Alençon's key religious building is the Church of Notre-Dame, which has a three-sided porch decorated with an admirable scene from the Transfiguration and a nave illuminated with wonderful stained-glass windows by master glaziers of Alençon and Maine.

Opposite the Maison d'Ozé, you can visit the house and bedroom where Thérèse Martin, St. Theresa of Lisieux, was born in 1873.

At the gateway to the *Alpes Mancelles* to the south of Alençon, the old bridge, gardens and setting of the village of Saint-Céneri-le-Gérei have attracted many artists. So has the Romanesque church, whose recently-restored frescoes are the oldest in Normandy, and the rustic Chapel of Saint-Céneri, a destination for pilgrims come to worship the Italian saint who founded the abbey in the 7th century.

Above
The town hall of Alençon, a fine building with a curved façade, was built between 1783 and 1795 according to plans drawn up by the architect Delarue.

Left page
These two imposing crenellated towers used to protect the entrance to the Château of the Dukes of Alençon, which was built in the 14th century and turned into a prison by Napoleon.

Right
In a tributary of the Sarthe, this 14th-century chapel is reputed to have been built on the oratory of Saint Céneri, a 7th-century Italian monk who founded the abbey which bears his name.

SÉES

Not many towns have been marked by history as much as Sées, located north of Alençon. Sées has been the seat of a bishopric since 400 AD. Religious institutions have thrived here for many years in the shadow of the bishops' palace. The cathedral, built in the 13th century, is its finest monument, even though the buttresses which had to be added to consolidate it have diminished the impact of its pure lines. According to specialists, it is "one of the last examples of Norman Gothic art", for tourism professionals it is the "star attraction of illuminated religious sites in the Orne". A sense of peace and contemplation comes over visitors upon penetrating the nave which, along with the transept and chancel, has retained all of its original purity. A summer festival, "Musilumières" showcases its exceptional acoustics.

Formerly the bishop's residence, the monumental *Palais d'Argentré*, built by the private tutor of Louis XVI, dates from the 18th century. The Abbey of Saint-Martin, the Renaissance-style Church of Notre-Dame-de-la-Place and the neo-Gothic Basilica de l'Immaculée-Conception make Sées a centre of Christianity and Christian art. Quite logically, the *département*'s Museum of Religious Art was installed here in the former canonical residence.

Below

The cathedral of Sées, illuminated.

THE FOREST OF ECOUVES

The road linking Sées to the west of the Orne runs along the Forest of Ecouves, one of the finest forests in the *département*, with its rugged landscape. This mix of broadleaf and coniferous trees covers some 14,000 hectares and is populated with large deer. The *Signal* of the Forest of Ecouves, the highest point in Normandy, rises above the foliage... Walkers meet at ancient crossroads, known as "stars", such as *Croix de Medavy*, *Croix Madame*, *Chêne au Verdier* and *Rochers du Vignage*, places with names that are still inscribed on ancient milestones.

At the entrance to the forest, the famous Château of Carrouges houses the offices of the Normandy-Maine regional nature park. This redbrick castle mixes the styles of Louis XIII and Henry IV. The pavilion in front of the entrance is more elegant, flanked by two towers topped with pepperboxes. A dark legend is attached to the castle, from which it is reputed to get its name: Karl le Rouge.

The Château of Couterne, on the road to Bagnoles-de-l'Orne, built in the 16th and 17th centuries, is more austere.

Opposite
The many forests of the Orne form a stunning backdrop to this *département*.

Below
The immense Château of Carrouges, which is accessed via this elegant pavilion.

BAGNOLES-DE-L'ORNE

Long ago, in the middle of Andaines, another marvellous forest, Hugues de Tessé discovered the curative properties of the water from the source of the river Vée. His horse and then he himself regained all their vigour after bathing here.

While this spot has seen many visitors seeking relief, Normandy's only spa resort, Bagnoles-de-l'Orne, is a more recent arrival, treating post-fractural problems and circulation and glandular disorders. On the other side of the lake, from the casino there emanates a sense of nostalgia for the Belle Epoque period of the early 20th century, when the resort's sumptuous villas were built.

A few sequoias have grown here among the no less majestic European species. Walk in the shadow of the trees and discover the legends of the *Saut du Capucin*, or Monk's Leap, and the *Roc au Chien*, or Rock of the Dog, which overlooks the town.

In Saint-Fraimbault, located at the edge of Maine and Normandy, choose one of several paths to discover the gardens and flowerbeds of this village, which won the National Flower Competition thanks to the work of its gardeners and inhabitants.

Above

The casino of Bagnoles-de-l'Orne nestles in a leafy setting, its white stone reflected in a wonderfully romantic lake.

DOMFRONT

The middle ages and wars of religion were periods of great unrest for Domfront, the stronghold of the counts of Bellême, built 70 metres above the Varenne river. Domfront came under English rule when it was taken by Henry I Beauclerc. Eleanor of Aquitaine and Henry Plantagenet stayed here, surrounded by a magnificent court. During the Hundred Years' War, it was besieged in turn by both French and English. Finally, in 1574, Gabriel de Montgomery, leader of the Huguenots who held it at that time, was forced to surrender to the Maréchal de Matignon, leader of the Catholics, before being executed on the orders of Catherine de Médicis.

Of its past, Domfront has retained a ditch, the remains of two of its keep walls and the base of two towers. The Duke of Sully destroyed the fortress built on the site of the garden, which contains the ruins of the Chapel of Saint-Symphorien. Restored ancient houses and shop fronts give Domfront a mediaeval feel. In this environment, the concrete belltower of the Church of Saint-Julien is surprising. Built in 1924 in Neo-Byzantine style, the interior layout of this sanctuary, which is decorated with a fine fresco of Christ in Majesty, is astonishing.

At the foot of the town, Notre-Dame-sur-l'Eau is the church which belonged to a priory of the Benedictine Abbey in Lonlay-l'Abbaye, located just a few miles away. Sadly, in the 19th century, most of the church's bays were removed to make way for a road.

Crossing Passais, of which Domfront is the capital, you will notice that apple orchards often give way to pear trees, and the no less sparkling perry takes the place of cider. One of the curiosities of Passais is the tower of Bonvouloir in Juvigny-sous-Andaine, which supposedly symbolises the virility of the lord who had it built. Evil be to him who evil thinks or, as the French put it: *Honni soit qui mal y pense*! In this land of countryside and forest, metallurgy once played a major role. The *Parc des Forges de Varennes* in Champsecret, where a blast furnace, Walloon forge and foundry have been restored, and the site of the ironworks in Champ-de-la-Pierre bear witness to the importance of this industry.

Below
The ruins of the Château of Domfront built in the 11th century by Henry I Beauclerc, destroyed, after many sieges, on the orders of Sully in 1608.

Below
The Church of Notre-Dame-sur-l'Eau, built in the 11th century. Several of the bays of this jewel of Romanesque architecture were destroyed in the 19th century to make way for a road.

FLERS

Flers was once a bastion of the counter-revolution in the *Bocage Normand*. Its leader, Louis de Frotté, shot in Verneuil-sur-Avre in 1800, set up his headquarters in the 18th-century Château of Flers, which is now home to the town hall and a museum which tells the story.

Above

A pretty park surrounds the Château of Flers, headquarters of the Counter-Revolutionaries during the French Revolution, now the town hall and Musée du Bocage.

THE ROCHE D'OËTRE

From Flers, Head Towards Putanges-Pont-Ecrepin, a gateway to Swiss Normandy, shared between Orne and Calvados. In Rabodanges, the 17th-century castle is reflected by the man-made lake on the Orne; 10 miles of this river's banks can be visited by boat. Downriver, beyond the gorges of Saint-Aubert, the Roche d'Oëtre stands 118 metres above the ravine where the Rouvre flows. This cliff of sandstone and pudding stone, interspersed with broom and scrub, is surrounded by some wild-looking woods. From certain angles, the cliff seems to resemble a human face. The summit can easily be accessed from the road on the other side, but take care when leaning out over this "Norman abyss"!

Hiking trails have been marked out starting from this site, one of the most original in Normandy. Several houses provide information and can be used as stopping-off points.

A museum has also been set up in Saint-Philbert-sur-Orne where visitors can learn about the lowest and oldest of France's mountains, the Armorican Massif.

ARGENTAN

Each to her own needlework! Argentan lace is different from Alençon lace. Take a careful look in the *Maison des Dentelles*, which tells the story of lace-making, or in Notre-Dame Abbey, where the tradition of lace-making lives on. Designed under Colbert, the secret of Argentan needlepoint lace was lost. Fortunately, it was rediscovered at the end of the 19th century and its originality saved. The château, seat of the courthouse, its chapel and the churches of Saint-Germain and Saint-Martin make up the architectural heritage of this sub-prefecture of the Orne, capital of the *Pays d'Argentan*, a land of pasture, tillage and forests, such as Gouffern and Petit Gouffern.

In Saint-Christophe-le-Jajolet, motorists who come to seek the protection of the patron saint of travellers will also discover the Château of Sassy with its famous terraced gardens. On the banks of the Orne, behind its remarkable towers and surrounded by grounds and a moat, lies the Château of Medavy. Nearby, in Mortrée, the pointed roofs, delicately decorated high windows and chequer-board façades of another noble residence are reflected in its lake. Many consider the Château d'O, built in the 16th century by Jean d'O and redesigned several times, to be the finest and most elegant in all Normandy. François d'O, superintendent of finances and a favourite of Henry III, is said to have gone bankrupt adding improvements to it.

In August 1944 American and Canadian troops came together at the enormous keep of Chambois, thus blocking the route of the 7th German army. Two days later, the German army surrendered in Tournai-sur-Dives. A monument on Mont Ormel recalls the part played in this victory by Polish soldiers fighting under Canadian command. The nearby village of Villebodin is home to the elegant 15th- and 16th-century *Manoir d'Argentelles*.

Below
The magnificently preserved square keep of Chambois is a fine example of military architecture. It was also one of the major sites of the Battle of Normandy.

HARAS DU PIN STUD FARM

Every year, thousands of horse-lovers visit Haras du Pin, the largest stud farm in France. Attracted here by races, displays of stallions and horse teams, the many visitors are also drawn by a visit to the tack room, saddlery and various outhouses containing barouches, breaks, hackneys, landaus and other carriages from a time when horses ruled the roads.

The naturalist and writer, Buffon, said of the horse "its resting place is a place of delight". Everything in the Haras du Pin has been designed to ensure that this is true. Jean-Baptiste Colbert created the national system of stud farms in 1665 in order to restrict imports. However the Haras du Pin stud farm was not built until 1715 and almost disappeared during the French Revolution. Nicknamed "the Versailles for horses", the stud farm houses around eighty stallions in its sumptuous stables, laid out in a semicircle around the main courtyard, the *Cour Colbert*. These stallions are responsible for siring eleven different horse breeds.

Set in parkland of almost 1,200 hectares, its long avenues bordered with ancient trees and gardens designed by Le Nôtre, the surroundings of Haras du Pin also attract many visitors.

Below

The Château of Haras du Pin was built according to plans drawn up by Jules Hardouin-Mansart, architect of Versailles, and may be visited at certain times of year alongside the stud farm.

PAYS D'AUGE ORNAIS COUNTRY

The *pays d'Auge Ornais* country is well known to food-lovers but before reaching its capital Vimoutiers, stop awhile in Gacé. This was the childhood home of Marie Duplessis (born near Bayeux), who inspired Alexandre Dumas to write *The Lady of the Camellias*, providing literature, opera and cinema with one of its most romantic heroines. A small museum in the town hall keeps her memory alive.

Vimoutiers, a small town on the river Vie, honours rather a different character. Despite the donation by an American cheese-making firm of a statue to Vimoutiers, many of those who appreciate her invention have never heard of Marie Harel, the farmer's wife who used the name of her village to name the most famous of cheeses: camembert. In Camembert itself, two museums, one housed in a renovated 13th-century farm, the second in a building whose architecture is reminiscent of the very form of the cheese, together with some farms, are devoted to the history of this product and reveal the procedures involved in its production as well as giving visitors a chance to sample the cheese itself.

A short distance away, the Priory of Saint-Michel-de-Crouttes, built between the 13th and 18th centuries, offers a happy, lasting image of the Orne. Its rose garden, arbour, medicinal herb garden, kitchen garden and tithe barn give an idea of what it was like to live and work in an abbey.

Below
Camembert, the cheese which made the fame of the *Pays d'Auge* country and Normandy. Napoleon III was responsible for its popularity, but Thomas Corneille had mentioned it two centuries earlier.

Eure

Cross the Eure *département* from east to west on the N13 road. This *département* is one vast plain, broken up, here and there, by a row of poplar trees, hiding a church steeple, and dotted with the odd village where the houses are built along the roadside.

Left page
Behind this wall stands the Abbey of Bec-Hellouin, founded in 1035 by Herluin. It was immortalised by Lanfranc and Anselme before being re-occupied by monks in 1948.

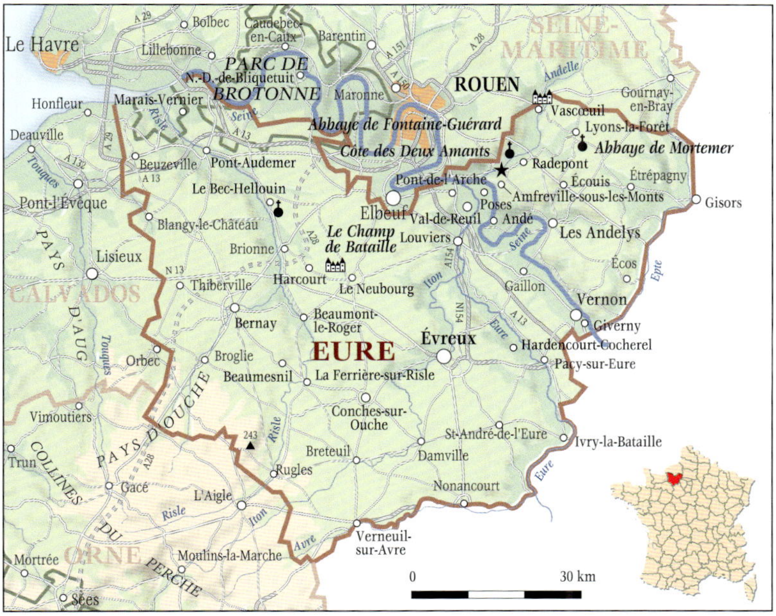

Much of Eure's charm is found in its gentle valleys, such as the Avre and the Epte, which border the *département* to the east and south. Unlike the Andelle which flows its own course, the Seine, Eure (and its tributary, the Iton) and Risle – which the Charentonne flows into – run from south to north, dividing the *département's* 2,332 square miles of territory into virtually equal portions of land. These rivers once served as water highways, and for years, their waters powered mill wheels and boats. Many of this département's wonders are to be found in its sunken valleys and on its hillsides.

Eure suffers the drawbacks and reaps the benefits of its proximity to Paris and its suburbs. It is more built up and industrialised in the east and in the Seine and Eure valleys where the majority of its 542,000 inhabitants are concentrated, while remaining more rural in the west. 127,000 hectares of woodland cover the region. According to the writer, Jean de La Varende, the Eure "is a reflection of all that the Norman *départements* have to offer". Today, in its tranquil areas, Eure is the ideal place to come for peace and relaxation.

The towns and villages of Les Andelys, Le Bec, Cocherel and Ivry are laden with history and artists have made Giverny an important centre of impressionist art.

THE UPPER VALLEY OF THE EURE

Pacy-sur-Eure, with its Church of Saint-Aubin boasting stained-glass windows and a high altar, was for a long time the first stop off point in Normandy for Parisians heading for the coast. The town makes the ideal place to set off on a hike through the upper valley of the Eure. Head towards Ivry-la-Bataille and visit the ruins of the 10th-century fortress and the obelisk standing midfield. This monument was built, under Napoleon's orders, to commemorate a battle, which is more famous for Henry IV's battle cry: "Let my white panache be your rallying point!", than for the victory that was won there over the members of the League. Along the river, two towns have museums devoted to their main industry, either now or in the past: the manufacture of combs in Ezy-sur-Eure and wind instrument-making in La Couture-Boussey. Cocherel, a pretty village downstream of Pacy, is featured in all the French history books.

In was in fact in Cocherel that Du Guesclin defeated the "English" troops of Charles the Bad, the King of Navarre, in 1364. Cocherel is also famous for another reason: a monument on the water's edge, *Les Méditations*, indicates that the village was the favourite residence of Aristide Briand, the relentless "Apostle of Peace", who is buried in the nearby cemetery.

Below

Last century, this old house, built on the foundations of the old bridge of Vernon, was restored in the style of a typical Normandy thatched cottage.

VERNON

The Seine, which, at this point, has just entered Normandy, stretches out to Vernon between a few islands and the foundations of an old bridge. This rustic town, which spreads out on either side of the river, seems an ideal place to live. In June, the air is fragrant with the scent of the many lime trees that line the town's avenues.

As Vernon was a good point at which to cross the Seine, it was fortified by Rollo. However, for the same reason, it suffered heavy bombing in 1944 by the Allies who sought to destroy its bridges. Henry I of England began the building work on the *Tour des Archives* on the left bank of the river, but it was under Philippe Auguste that the work was completed. The Château des Tournelles, built in the 12th century, stands on the right bank and once protected the bridge whose foundations can still be seen emerging from the waters. An old house stands above them, unaware of the passage of time. On the left bank, in among the modern buildings, a few timber-framed houses, including one named *Temps jadis* (Times of old), have survived the ravages of time and war. Each period in history, from the 12th century through to the Renaissance, has taken turns rebuilding the Church of Notre-Dame. Its most noteworthy features include the rose window on the façade, and – inside the building – the triforium organ and stained-glass windows. Four 15th- and 19th-century dwellings house the A.G. Poulain museum whose pride and joy are the works of Pierre Bonnard and some works by Monet.

Home to the Ariane rocket engine manufacturer Snecma, Vernon is both a forward-looking and historical town. The Château de Bizy's grounds are located in the heart of the forest that stretches down to the river from Hameau de Normandie. Baroque-style fountains, with Neptune, lions, the character *Gribouille*, horses and dolphins rising up out of the water, embellish the listed park which was designed in the 18th century by Garnier d'Isle. Louis-Philippe redesigned the park in the English style and had many of its trees planted. The Château de Bizy was built in 1741 (according to Constant d'Ivry's plans) for the Duke of Belle-Ile, the grandson of Superintendent Fouquet, but has since changed hands many times. In 1858, Baron Shickler, the brother-in-law of Duke d'Albufera, the then mayor of Vernon, had the castle's central building rebuilt, leaving only the original stables intact. The result of his work is the beautiful white stone, Italian-style building which rises up in the centre of the main courtyard and now features tapestries, panelling and furniture, to the delight of art lovers.

GIVERNY

Monet's house and gardens were restored by Van der Kampf, their curator, in 1976. Claude Monet, who was born in Paris, but had close ties with Normandy after buying a barn there in which to set up his workshop, actually lived here from 1890 to 1926. Consequently, in a matter of decades, the village of Giverny, set on the banks of the Epte on the Normandy border, became the capital of impressionist art and one of Normandy's most visited centres of art and culture.

From spring to autumn, visitors flock to the large house with its pink

Below

Regardless of the season, gardeners strive to make Monet's gardens flourish in keeping with the spirit of the artist.

Opposite
Water lilies still flaunt their different shades of white on the pond in Monet's gardens in Giverny.

roughcast front, green shutters and slate roof to view the artist's everyday possessions and surprising collection of Japanese engravings. Most popular are the gardens which have been restored in keeping with the spirit of their creator, the tireless painter. Visitors love to lean over the little bridge to admire the white water lilies which still flower on the pond, flaunting those shades of colour that the artist so desperately sought to capture.

What was the lure of this place? Was it the clear skies or perhaps the proximity to Paris? After Monet settled in the town, American painters and hundreds of other young artists flocked to Giverny, where they made their homes and set up their easels. It is even said that Lily Cabot advised Monet about what seeds to buy for his garden. The Chicago Terra Foundation – founded by Daniel J. Terra and his wife Judith – opened the Museum of American Art in Giverny which is dedicated to American artists from Monet's time and all other artists throughout America's history. The pure lines of the museum's architecture, its plant-decked terraced roofs which blend in perfectly with the setting, its surrounding gardens, remarkable collections and conferences soon drew crowds in significant numbers.

Below
Museum of American Art in Giverny
Reichen & Robert, architects
Photos: N. Mathéus.

GISORS

An enormous fortress overlooks the town of Gisors which is set upstream of the river Epte. Standing on the border of the Normandy Vexin region, Gisors was once a lookout post over the kingdom of France. Built by William Rufus and reinforced by Henry Plantagenet, the town fell into the hands of Philippe Auguste in 1193. Five centuries later, Sully ordered its destruction but, much to the delight of military architecture enthusiasts, the orders were never carried out and the exemplary building was handed down through the ages, practically intact. The keep and watchtower, which are surrounded by the castle walls, defy all attack. Nevertheless, a group of over-zealous fortune seekers once almost caused the fortress to come crashing down when they searched its foundations for the hidden treasure of the Knights Templar – which, incidentally, was never discovered! The 13th- and 14th-century Church of Saint-Gervais-et-Saint-Protais is embellished with fine sculptures and stained-glass windows.

Opposite

The keep and watchtower of the Château de Gisors stand defiant. However, during the Hundred Years' War, the fortress changed hands several times.

Left page, top
Snow has covered the dovecote and monastic building of what was once a Cistercian abbey.

Left page, bottom left
The ruins of Mortemer abbey.

Left page, bottom right
In 1054, near Mortemer, the Duke of Normandy's troops surprised the King of France's men in their sleep. Clearly they could have done with a helping hand from the cackling geese that warned of a similar attack at the Capitol in ancient Rome!

ECOUIS

In 1054, In Mortemer near Lisors, William the Conqueror's troops surprised the King of France's men in their sleep (or perhaps in a drunken stupor). The King's army had invaded the duchy and massacred the town, according to legend. Today, there is nothing left to show that this battle ever took place. The undulating and peaceful setting does however feature an abbey (ruined for the most part). This houses a museum which, among other things, tells the story of Norman legends and ghosts.

In the nearby village of Ecouis, the collegiate Church of Notre-Dame was founded by Enguerrand de Marigny, the Superintendent of Philippe le Bel, who was the victim of a conspiracy and ended his life hanging from the Montfaucon gallows. Statues of Christ, Our Lady of Ecouis, Saint Cécile, Saint Marguerite, Saint Nicaise, Saint Mary Magdalene – with her long, flowing hair – and members of the Marigny family date from the 14th and 15th centuries and make this church popular with sculpture lovers.

Below
The 14th- and 15th-century statues of the nave and chancel in the collegiate Church of Ecouis are well worth a visit.

LYONS-LA-FORÊT

Lyons certainly deserves its title of one of France's most beautiful villages. Fittingly, ten thousand hectares of forest surround the village. After admiring its covered market – a carpenters' masterpiece – and the old dwellings, wander through the long alleys to the arboretum which features one of France's finest beech groves or head for one of the hamlets hidden in the forest clearings.

To the west of the forest, the clear waters of the rivers Crevon and Heron flow through the grounds of the Château de La Forestière with its monumental dovecote. Jules Michelet was once a guest at the Château de Vascœuil, which is now the headquarters of a contemporary art centre. It was here that the historian wrote part of his *Histoire de France* in which he described his love for the owner, Mme Dumesnil. But her death soon put a stop to his passion. A few objects, manuscripts and souvenirs, exhibited in the castle's small museum, tell the tale of his stay at Vascœuil.

Below
" [...] an enormous dovecote for such a small house", wrote Michelet in his diary, referring to the Château de Vascœuil, nowadays an arts centre featuring a museum dedicated to the historian.

THE CÔTE DES DEUX AMANTS

A curse seems to fall on all love affairs, whether actual or fictional, that begin in this corner of the world. Follow a small road that winds its way round the hill and after a few more steps you will reach Amfreville-sous-les-Monts at the top of the Côte des Deux Amants hill. The view is superb, but after admiring the Seine valley, look back down the hill and spare a thought for the tragic tale of the King of Pîtres' daughter and her lover as told by Marie de France:

Once upon a time in Normandy,
So the well-known story goes,
Two young people fell in love...

In order to win the daughter's hand from her father the King, the young man, aided by a love potion, carried his lover from the depth of the valley to the top of this hill. But the effort killed him and the daughter died of grief. The Abbey of Notre-Dame-de-Fontaine-Guérard, founded in the 12th century, stands at the foot of the hill, in Radepont, at the edge of the river Andelle. Its abbey church is in ruins, but the Chapel of Saint-Michel, the chapter house and the Cistercian monks' workroom remain intact. The monastery's stones were used to build a mill (in a mock mediaeval style) but shortly after the building work was completed, the mill was destroyed by fire.

Above
"[...] scarcely have you penetrated the dark shadows of the cursed mill than the Abbaye de Fontaine-Guérard comes into view." Philippe Delerm, *Les chemins nous inventent.*

POSES

Geography, civil engineering, wildlife and a leisure centre: just before leaving the Eure *département* to enter Seine-Maritime, the Seine forms a loop around an area that features a number of interesting places. Maupassant himself wrote about the construction of the Amfreville-sous-les-Monts locks which witness the passing of boats travelling up and down the Seine, to and from Paris. A museum depicts the various aspects and history of navigation on this river which you can cross on the Poses dam above the swirling waters below. Upstream, some large quarries have been converted into Normandy's largest open-air leisure centre. The Normandy ornithological group has made the *Réserve de la Grande Noé*, based on the site, a viewing spot for observing migratory birds and other waterside birds, which flock here in vast numbers.

Nearby, as elsewhere, Normandy plays on its contrasts. Visitors can make up their own mind about the Parisian deconcentration policy when they visit Val-de-Reuil, one of the towns built for this purpose around forty years ago. In stark contrast, Pont-de-l'Arche, where the Eure meets the Seine, is an ancient town. Fortified with ramparts and ditches, whose remains can still be seen, it was built at the first possible crossing

Left

At the gates of Pont-de-l'Arche, the Abbey of Bonport, built to fulfil a wish of Richard the Lionheart, was given its rightful place along the historic Normandy abbey trail.

point over the Seine. A stained-glass window in Notre-Dame-des-Arts illustrates how difficult it was for the boatmen to negotiate the arch of the fortified bridge that defended the town. Near the town gates, the Cistercian Abbey of Bonport, which was built to fulfil a wish of Richard the Lionheart after he narrowly escaped drowning nearby, has been given its rightful place along the historic Normandy abbey trail.

Just upstream, on the right bank of the Seine, the mill of Andé, a very pretty 12th century, timber-framed building, features a hanging wheel and is the last remaining mill of its kind in Europe. Its owner has turned it into a cinema and music centre.

LOUVIERS

Louviers, where Mendès France was mayor, for many years vied with its neighbour, Elbeuf, for the title of "Cloth capital of Normandy". This rivalry became futile with the decline of the industry, whose golden days are recounted in the town's museum. Nowadays it is difficult to imagine that the many branches of the river that flow through the town were once used for shipping by the spinning and weaving industries. It is doubtless for this reason that Louviers is the only town in Europe to have cloisters (belonging to the Penitents' Convent) built alongside a river. A short distance away, the south wall and the porch of the Church of Notre-Dame bear witness to the talent of sculptors and stone-carvers from the days when Flamboyant style was at its peak. The nave, which is decorated in a more denuded Gothic style, is embellished with 15th- and 16th-century statues and features the tomb recess of Robert d'Acquigny, a local lord. The fact that the Louviers weavers contributed one of the stained-glass windows to the church testifies to the wealth and power of their trade in the late Middle Ages.

It is well worth taking a detour to the 16th century Château d'Acquigny located in the vicinity. The château stands in grounds that are at once classical, romantic and exotic in style. The wrought iron railings feature the initials of the names of those who built this beautiful castle.

Below

Built by Anne de Montmorency-Laval, the widow of Louis de Silly, in the 16th century, the Château d'Acquigny was extended with the addition of two wings in the 18th century.

Above
On 6 March 1204, the siege and cunning of the troops of the King of France, Philippe Auguste, enabled the men to take possession of the castle, built by Richard the Lionheart eight years earlier.

LES ANDELYS

Further upstream of the Seine, Grand Andely and Petit Andely formed the town of Les Andelys – a sub-prefecture of the Eure *département*. Château-Gaillard, one of the most famous historic buildings in Normandy, towers above the town from the top of a chalk cliff, which is pierced with the entrances to deep caves.

Richard the Lionheart returned from his crusade to discover that his brother John had given up the duchy to the King of France. He vowed to win it back and built this fortress in 1196. It is protected, on one side, by the cliff on which it stands, and, on the other side, by deep trenches, a stronghold and ramparts. From the middle of the platform, the central tower, which is reinforced by a keep, stands as if impregnable. It was not long before Richard exclaimed: "Isn't my one year old daughter beautiful!" But when, in 1203, Philippe Auguste attacked it, Richard, who had been killed while besieging the Château de Châlus, was no longer there to defend his fortress. In February 1204, after huge siege efforts, the French took possession of the castle via the latrines. Its defenders did not even have time to take refuge in the keep. The duchy met its end at Château-Gaillard, followed by Rouen which capitulated a few weeks later. When exploring its ruins, native Normans would surely love to rewrite this chapter in history, and visitors cannot help but admire the somewhat madcap courage of the castle's attackers.

Thus the impregnable fortress fell into the hands of the Kings of France; however, it was not destroyed until much later under the orders of Henry IV, and then of Cardinal Richelieu. Some of its stones were reused to build the summer palace for the Rouen Archbishops in Gaillon. In the meantime, the castle suffered many other attacks and Louis le Hutin had his wife, Marguerite de Bourgogne, imprisoned there before she was strangled to death. From the walls of Château-Gaillard, the view stretches out over the magnificent Seine valley. At the foot of the wall, the domed bell tower of the Church of Saint-Jacques, the slender spire of the Church of Saint-Sauveur and the majestic towers of Notre-Dame can be seen rising up from among Les Andelys rooftops. These buildings are all worth visiting, as is the museum of Nicolas-Poussin, the great artist who was born in 1594 in Villers, near Les Andelys. Don't forget to throw a coin into the fountain where, so legend has it, Saint Clotilde changed the water into wine to quench the thirst of the masons who built the church.

Below
Petit Andely, on the bank of the Seine, and Grand Andely, in the valley of Cambon, formed Les Andelys. The slender steeple of the Church of Saint-Sauveur rises up above the town.

EVREUX

Evreux is the Eure *departement's* prefecture, an industrial town and a major agricultural centre. It is also a bishopric, of which the illustrious Du Perron was appointed Bishop in 1591 and Cardinal thirteen years later. The portrait of an Evreux citizen who lived in the 4th century, along with the thermal baths, restored and on display, of the holy Gallo-Roman city of Gisacum, located in the neighbouring town of Vieil-Evreux, bear witness to the distant past of this capital of the Eure, a past marred by tragedy. Evreux was set alight and ransacked by the Vandals, the Vikings, Henry I of England, Philippe Auguste, John the Good and Charles V, and bombed by the Germans in 1940 and then again on various occasions by the Allies.

The promenade along the river Iton, which runs through the town, will take you inside the ramparts, which have surrounded Evreux ever since the Gallo-Roman era and where you can discover the town's most interesting features. At night, the spotlights reveal Notre Dame's lantern tower, spire and nave. Looking down from the heights of Côte Saint-Michel or Côte de Paris, the whole town appears to huddle round the sanctuary which was rebuilt many times between the 10th and 18th centuries and restored in more recent times. The northern transept and its door are doubtless the cathedral's most beautiful architectural features and the detail of the paling on the side chapels and the seventy windows from the 12th, 14th and 15th centuries, which shed light on the chancel and nave, are pure works of art.

Nearby, the Episcopal palace, built in the 15th century, has been converted into the town museum and its archaeology section is of particular interest. Walk through the town centre to discover the town hall and theatre in their beautiful green setting. Opposite these two buildings, which are typical of late 19th century architecture, the slender and elegant silhouette of a 15th-century belfry towers above the modern apartment blocks, adding a mediaeval touch to the town. The Abbey Church of Saint-Taurin is set along the road leading to the outlying district of Navarre. It was built in 660, and conceals a treasure from the Middle Ages – a gilt silver shrine, decorated with precious stones, which contains the remains of the first Bishop of Evreux.

Above

Evreux Cathedral's windows, which have escaped the devastation of war, are, along with the panelling around the nave, one of the sanctuary's most beautiful adornments.

Right page

The promenades along the river Iton offer some outstanding views of the cathedral.

CONCHES

It was undoubtedly Roger de Tosny who gave Conches its name when he brought a relic of Saint Foy – a celebrated young martyr – back from Conques, a famous pilgrimage site in the Aveyron *département*. Roger de Tosny in fact founded the settlement of Conches, which is today a pretty village nestling 144 metres above the river Rouloir. Featuring a keep, modern statues on the main square, half-timbered houses, art workshops and public gardens, Conches is above all famous for its stained-glass windows and glass, the subject of a museum in the town. Most of the twenty-two stained-glass windows in the Church of Sainte-Foy date from the early Renaissance period and were created by the great master, Arnoult de Nimègue, and Romain Buron. The intense blues and reds, the depictions of the Last Supper and the Virgin with Saint Adrian and Saint Romain and the symbolisation of the Eucharist mystery – *Le Pressoir mystique* (meaning "the mystical winepress") – are the finest works in this collection.

Above

The keep and ruins of Conches castle, built by Roger de Tosny, overlook Rouloir valley.

VERNEUIL-SUR-AVRE

The Verneuil-sur-Avre coat of arms bears the inscription "ONQUES N'EST CLOS" (meaning "never closed") and displays an eye as its emblem. The town was in fact the centrepiece along the Avre defence line which protected the duchy of Normandy and, during the Hundred Years' War, it separated the English from the French until 1449 when it finally became French. Built by Philippe Auguste, the *Tour Grise* is the main relic from this distant past.

The ancient waterways that weave their way through the town are the result of work by Henry Beauclerc. Verneuil was short of water to fill its moats and ditches and as the Avre ran through French land, Beauclerc diverted the Iton which flowed 6 miles away.

Taller than the *Tour Grise* – a stern-looking keep – the four storeys of the Church of La Madeleine's tower rise 60m above Verneuil and are sometimes compared to Rouen's *Tour de Beurre*.

The church's stained-glass windows, many statues and a Van Loo painting add to its architectural features. A cenotaph was also built there in memory of Louis de Frotté, head of the *Chouan* counter-revolutionaries. Nearby, Notre-Dame features sculptures from the School of Verneuil. Statues of the *Vierge à la Pomme*, the *Vierge Dolente*, Saint Denis, Saint James and Saint Christopher testify to the talent of the stone and wood sculptors.

Many perfectly restored, half-timbered or stone houses line the streets, adding to the town's charm.

Top, right
The wealth and finery of the sculptures in the 60 metre-tall tower of the Church of La Madeleine in Verneuil-sur-Avre meant that it is often compared to Rouen Cathedral's *Tour de Beurre*.

Opposite
This old building in Verneuil-sur-Avre has a beautiful chequered façade.

BEAUMESNIL

The landscape of the *pays d'ouche* country may appear stark and severe at first glance. Yet fields and meadows are interspersed with woods, and dotted with copses shielding old marl pits. The forests of Conches, Breteuil and Beaumont also cover the area. When passing through them at night in the autumn, you can hear the call of stags living in the thickets.

Discover La Ferrière on the Conches to Bernay road. The village appears to be sleeping between its 14th-century covered market and chequered-wall church, set on the banks of the Risle. A few miles away, on flat terrain this time, in the centre of another equally peaceful village, a white limestone and pink brick façade, with a kind of lantern tower on the roof, rises up at the end of an alleyway. Jean de La Varende, who is buried nearby in Chamblac, based the "Mesnil Royal" castle in his book *Nez de cuir* on the Château de Beaumesnil – a fine example of Louis XIII-style architecture. This large castle now houses a bookbinding museum. The surrounding French-style gardens, designed by La Quintinie, feature ornamental pools and fountains, the *Jardin de Madame* and an aisle of lime trees. An enormous boxwood maze – a popular attraction among 18th century gardeners – still flourishes there, inviting you to lose your way.

Opposite
"No other Louis XIII building in France is so beautiful", wrote Jean de La Varende in *Nez de cuir*, referring to the Château de Beaumesnil.

BEAUMONT-LE-ROGER

Between Beaumesnil and Le Neubourg, Beaumont-le-Roger is one of those pretty villages dotted along the course of the Risle that only come to life at weekends. The Church of Saint Nicolas, set amid idyllic scenery, was restored to its original design after the war. Its bell tower, where the clockwork figure of Régulus ceaselessly marks out the hours, rises up on the hillside, overlooking the square and the main street. The romantic ruins of the *Abbaye de la Trinité* can be seen further down the same hillside, and it is easy to picture the fortress wall, which may have been built by Roger de Beaumont, standing long ago behind the arcades. At the bottom of the valley, the river and its branches flow round the back of the houses and their little gardens and across a few small meadows before converging beneath the arches of an old bridge.

Above
The ruins of the *Prieuré de la Trinité* overlook the little town of Beaumont-le-Roger from the Risle valley hillside.

LE NEUBOURG

Beaumont stretches out along the river while the town of Le Neubourg lies at the heart of the vast and fertile Neubourg plain. In the town centre, the 16th-century Church of Saint-Pierre-et-Saint-Paul looks out onto a square which is still too narrow to contain the market.

Formerly protected by ramparts, traces of which can still be seen, Le Neubourg has always been a major agricultural centre. The colourful, lively and plentiful market, full of local produce (*fois gras* four times a year), is well worth a visit. An interesting, unusual attraction is the *Musée de l'Ecorché d'Anatomie*, where paper mâché models created by Dr. Auzoux for medical schools are on display. Nearby, 138 hectares of recently-restored French-style parks and gardens surround the Château du Champ de Bataille, a magnificent 17th-century building, whose décor and furniture evoke a lifestyle more typical of that of the 18th century. The mediaeval, less refined and defensive Château d'Harcourt, birthplace of an important French family, is located in the centre of France's oldest arboretum, founded in 1826. Some four hundred ligneous species grow there.

Above
Built as a fortress in the 12th century and redesigned in the 17th century, the Château d'Harcourt has preserved its military allure. The surrounding arboretum is the oldest in France and features an impressive number of species.

Opposite
138 hectares of parks and gardens surround the Château du Champ-de-Bataille which easily measures up to Neubourg plain.

BEC-HELLOUIN ABBEY

A tall and gracious tower rises up out of the greenery of a valley whose "bec", or stream, flows towards the Risle. An elegant balustrade circles the top of the tower which is surmounted by a small pinnacle. This is Saint-Nicolas tower, the last remains of the Church of Bec-Hellouin, one of Normandy's largest abbeys. The abbey was founded in 1034 by Herluin, a knight who had grown weary of fighting and traded in his armour for a monk's habit. From its very origins, the abbey played an important political and religious role in what was then the embryo of Europe, created by William the Conqueror, in the duchy, England and Italy. Lanfranc, a theologian and religious man from Pavia, and the abbey's first prior, became the close ally and adviser to William the Conqueror when he laid siege to Brionne, a local town on the river Risle which is overlooked by the ruins of a keep. Lanfranc, who was the first abbot of Saint-Etienne in Caen, later became the Archbishop of Canterbury but kept up close relations with Bec-Hellouin. Anselme, Lanfranc's successor from Val d'Aoste, played a key role in promoting the intellectual influence of the monastery.

The abbey was virtually deserted during the French Revolution before being abandoned to the pickaxes of material merchants, and any rooms that were spared were used as a cavalry depot. The 15th-century Saint-Nicolas tower, a few pillar bases and the remains of the southern transept are all that remain of one of the largest abbey churches ever built. The monastic buildings suffered far less damage. The cloister, monastic hostelry, abbey lodge and refectory – nowadays the church – restored in the 17th century by Maurist monks, are a remarkable example of classical architecture, masterminded by Guillaume de La Tremblaye, an architect and monk at Bec abbey and master builder in Caen.

With the return of the Benedictine monks in 1948, the abbey took up its former vocation as a place of prayer and retreat, and also one of research and exchange. In the new abbey church the abbey's founder lies in a sarcophagus before the high altar, which was donated by the Aoste region.

Below

Rising up out of the greenery, Saint-Nicolas tower is the only remains of the church of the famous Bec-Hellouin Abbey, a working abbey located in the centre of a delightful village.

BERNAY

Bernay is one of the few Norman towns whose centre was spared by war. The centre has been redesigned and rendered more cheerful and gives this Eure sub-prefecture an undeniable character and air of authenticity. Many antique shops have opened up there. Its numerous timber-framed or rubble stone and flint houses line the banks of the river Charentonne or its tributary, the Cosnier. Neglected for centuries, the abbey is now once again a historic Norman heritage site. Founded in 1013 by Judith de Bretagne, the wife of Richard II, under the management of Guillaume de Volpiano – the famous Abbot of Fécamp – the abbey is considered to be

the birthplace of Romanesque art in Normandy. The monastic buildings are now home to the town hall, and the abbey lodge houses the Fine Arts museum with its collections of pottery and ceramics from Rouen.

The Church of Sainte-Croix is adorned with some remarkable works of art, some of them originating from Bec. The nave and chancel contain tombstones and statues of apostles and evangelists and the high altar features the nativity scene. For some time, the Basilica of Notre-Dame-de-la-Couture, with its wooden archways and magnificent stained-glass windows, has played host to a religious Norman brotherhood on Pentecost Monday.

Homeland of the poet Alexandre – the inventor of the alexandrine verse – Bernay was also the home of the members of the Convention, Thomas and Robert Lindet. The *Promenade des Monts* offers a superb view of the town.

Right
The restored abbey church, founded in Bernay by Judith de Bretagne, the grandmother of William the Conqueror, is a fine example of Romanesque art.

MARAIS VERNIER MARSHES

Pont-Audemer's bridges, streets and typical dwellings, built along the Risle, have earned this town the title of "Venice of Normandy". For centuries, it has been the region's tanning and paper-making capital, and is appropriately set between the river Eure and the Seine estuary. The Church of Saint-Ouen, built in the 11th century and enlarged in the 16th century, which features some remarkable furnishings, is adorned with magnificent stained-glass windows from the Renaissance period and also modern stained-glass windows designed by Max Ingrand.

Cross the A13 towards the Tancarville suspension bridge – the oldest engineering structure in the lower Seine valley – to reach the Marais Vernier marshes. From the 180 or 90 B-road, and the *Pointe de la Roque* headland, there is a magnificent panoramic view which stretches out over the marshland – one of Normandy's most famous natural attractions.

This highly original, man-made area dates from the days of Henry IV when the land, which was all too often inundated by the sea, was dried out for farming. The Dutch arrived somewhat later to complete the work and a dyke, built in 1607, between the *Bout d'Aval* and Saint-Aubin canal, has been named after them. Today, conservation work is being carried out to preserve the original character of the marshes – wetlands, which are essential for the protection of wildlife and flora.

The villages of Sainte-Opportune-la-Mare, Bouquelon, Quillebeuf-sur-Seine, Saint-Samson, Marais Vernier, Vieux-Port and Aizier make ideal starting points for setting off and discovering the 5,000 hectares that make up France's largest peat bog and an ecological area which is recognised on a European scale. Between the patchwork of meadows and wetlands, where the slightest breeze rustles the reeds, and between the dykes and orchards, the grass grows greener than hope itself, as the saying goes. Apple trees and thatched cottages are typical sights in the area. Purple and blue irises flourish thick and fast on the tops of clay walls. The herds around the *Grande Mare*, in the Manneville reserve, have different coats and shapes from those of the heavier and stronger Norman breeds; dark Scottish bulls and Camargue horses are better suited to these waterlogged soils. The Marais Vernier marshes provide a refuge to thousands of nesting and migrating birds, much to the delight of birdwatchers. Similarly, the variety of plant species that grow there are a joy to botanists.

Roumois, another Norman area, is located to the east of the marshes.

Above

Narrow streets, half-timbered houses, the reaches of various rivers and Pont-Audemer's old town are simply picturesque in the shade of Saint-Ouen's bell tower.

Likewise, this area (or at least some of it) forms part of the *Parc naturel régional des Boucles de la Seine Normande*. The 50,000 hectares of this nature park stretch across Eure and Seine-Maritime encompassing some fifty towns from these two *départements*. Roumois became better known by reviving old trades, ancient activities and traditional regional events. Visit, for instance, Hauville windmill, the bread oven and clog museum in La Haye-de-Routot, the linen museum in Routot and a traditional mill in Saint-Ouen-de-Pontcheuil. However, perhaps this region's oldest witnesses to the past are the two, thousand-year-old yew trees in La Haie-de-Routot which both harbour chapels and have 16-and 14-metre trunks. The *Maison du Parc* is set in Notre-Dame-de-Bliquetuit in a very beautiful old manor-style farmhouse. On the border between Eure and Calvados, at the gateway to the *Pays d'Auge* country, two small towns in this *département* are well worth a visit for tourists in Haute Normandie: the traditional, picturesque town of Cormeilles, and Beuzeville, whose Church of Saint-Hélier boasts nineteen fine stained-glass windows by modern-day master stained glass maker, François Décorchemont.

Right
This residence, with irises on the ridge tiling, a thatched roof and clay walls, has been renovated using typical materials and architectural techniques from the Marais Vernier marshes.

Below
The slightest breeze rustles the Marais Vernier marshes where Camargue horses and Scottish bulls roam.

Seine-Maritime

Seine-Maritime is the birthplace of Normandy. When Rollo signed the Treaty of Saint-Clair-sur-Epte he was already settled in Rouen. Although William the Conqueror made Caen his capital, some of his most important decisions were made in Rouen where he died. Rouen's fall contributed just as much as that of Château-Gaillard to the end of the duchy's independence, but it was in Rouen that the Parliament of Normandy was based until it disappeared in 1775.

Left page
Etretat's cliffs and "doorways", undoubtedly one of Normandy's most popular sites and definitely one of Seine-Maritime's.

Its population of 1,240,000, nearly 520 people per square mile, and its influence on France's economy have made Seine-Maritime the most important *département* in Normandy. Its geography and its activities are wide and varied. The wooded and hilly landscape of the stock-farming *Pays de Bray* country is different from that of the *Pays de Caux* country, a plateau devoted to crop farming with high cliffs that drop sharply to the sea. Nearly 100,000 hectares of its 2,424 square mile area is woodland, which is mainly concentrated around the meanders of the river Seine between Rouen and Le Havre.

Although industrialised for centuries, Seine-Maritime is also a rich agricultural land. Le Havre and Rouen are considered to be among France's leading ports while Renaissance architecture and offshore fishing have made the those of Dieppe and Fécamp famous. Many seaside towns sprang up near Paris as a result of the popularity of sea bathing, which originated in Dieppe. Etretat, the most popular of them all, became famous for its cliffs.

Throughout the centuries, and even before the Normans arrived, Seine-Maritime's heritage has been like no other. Five of its towns are classified as "Towns of Art and History" while 207 historical monuments are listed here; more than 450 rank on France's *Inventaire supplémentaire*.

Different "routes" and "itineraries" meet here: spice, ivory, abbeys, impressionists, etc. Corneille, Flaubert, Maupassant, Gide, Géricault, Monet and Dufy have also contributed to the renown of this *département* through literature or art.

Below

The *tour Saint-Romain* with its axe blade shaped roof. On its left is the façade of Rouen cathedral and the *portail Saint-Jean* doorway.

ROUEN

Since the time of Arthur Young, the 19th-century explorer, it is widely acknowledged that Rouen is best discovered from a height. Sainte-Catherine coast offers the most famous view of this city. Maupassant's description of the city was from the coast of Canteleu viewpoint while André Maurois described it from the area surrounding Robert the Devil's castle.

The river Seine divides Rouen into two towns. On the right bank, the spire, the cathedral towers and the keep are emblems of a two thousand year old town. On the left bank, beyond the tower of Archives, stretches the industrial town of Saint-Sever which sprang up in the 18th century and is currently a commercial and administrative district.

Rarely do areas as small as that of the first town feature so many monuments. Bishops and religious orders played a major role in this phenomenon. A large part of Rouen's architectural heritage is religious although abbeys and churches were destroyed in the 19th century when *rue Thiers*, *rue Jeanne-d'Arc* and *rue de la République* were built by mayors Ambroise Fleury and Louis Verdrel. The Church of Saint-Amand was among those destroyed but three still remain in the heart of Rouen.

Notre-Dame cathedral, referred to as an "Important building of Haute-Normandie", and which almost disappeared in 1944, is the symbol of

Right page

Lengthy restoration work has revealed the full brilliance of Rouen cathedral's stone towers and façade.

Rouen's long existence. It was built on the site of a 4th-century basilica and consecrated in the presence of William the Conqueror in 1063. However, the current sanctuary was built from the 13th to 16th century. The 151-metre spire is the highest in France and its 9,000-tonne lantern tower was built in 1830.

The doorways of the *portail des Libraires* and the *portail de la Calende* and the west façade, flanked by the *tour Saint-Romain* and the *tour de Beurre*, which reveal authentic stone filigree and were often painted by Monet, are masterpieces. On the inside, the chancel with its simple design is a fine example of Gothic art. In the chapels, the tombs of Cardinals d'Amboise and Louis de Brézé and the recumbent statues of Rollo, Richard the Lionheart, Empress Matilda and the Duke of Bedford, which surround the chancel, have made Normandy a historical memorial.

Saint-Maclou porch, a few steps away from the cathedral, has no fewer than five arches along its façade. Construction of this spectacular Flamboyant church was undertaken during the English occupation in 1437 and was completed sixty years later. On the inside, marble columns that support the organ loft, rood loft stairs and the rood beam can be admired.

You can then visit the former cemetery of this parish, the *Aître Saint-Maclou*: a square courtyard with a cross standing in the centre and enclosed in a gallery of magnificently

Right page, top

Place du Vieux-Marché, where Joan of Arc was tortured and the pillars of the Church of Saint-Sauveur near the stake have been unearthed.

Opposite

As in days gone by – but undoubtedly clearer – the stream still runs through the middle of the rue *Eau-de-Robec* roadway.

Below

The Aître Saint-Maclou, which was the parish cemetery, is within a few steps of the Flamboyant church.

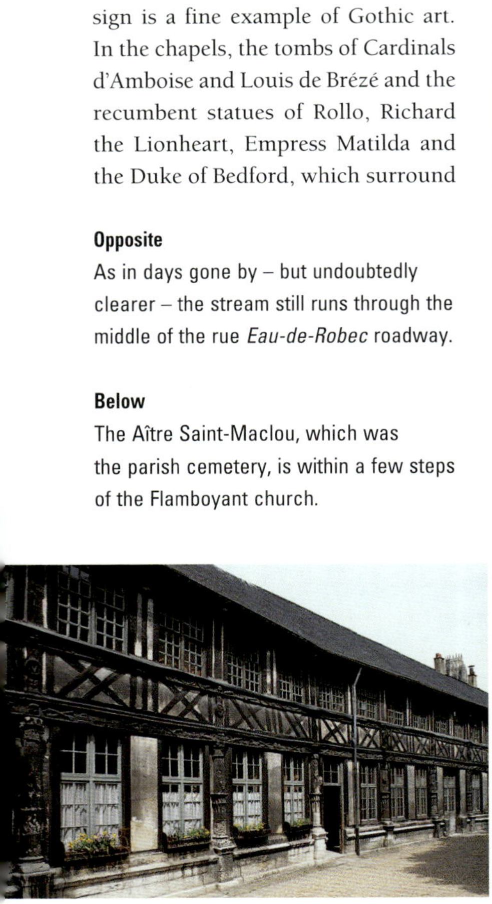

sculptured beams whose characters seem to be leading a gruesome dance. The remains of the dead were laid in its attics from the 14th to 18th centuries.

The course of the famous Rouen stream was returned to *rue Eau-de-Robec*, where it runs through the middle of the roadway. The chevet and the central tower or "Tour Couronnée" of Saint-Ouen, the third largest sanctuary in Rouen, rise up out of a garden. This garden can be reached by the *portail des Marmousets* with its impressive keystone. Saint-Ouen, the church of a monastery founded in the 7th century to house the relics of Rouen's Prelate, was built between the 14th and 16th centuries. It is somewhat bigger than the cathedral for which it is sometimes mistaken and has a particularly striking style.

Below, left
A small museum where waxworks evoke the life and death of the shepherd girl of Domrémy and thousands of works dedicated to her are displayed.

Below, right
The *Galerie du Souvenir* leading from the place du Vieux-Marché to the Church of Jeanne-d'Arc with its huge roof.

Despite the duration of the construction, the original plan was followed to the letter.

It shows beautiful harmony and luminosity with its refined columns, rose window and stained-glass windows. In the 19th century, the town hall was set up in the monastic buildings of the abbey, which, except for those with garden views, were often redesigned, particularly to make way for the current *place du Général-de-Gaulle*, which is decorated with a beautiful fountain and an unusual statue of Napoleon.

Among the other sanctuaries that make Rouen an important place for religious architecture are Saint-Romain, where a red marble sarcophagus contains the relics of the Prelate who became the patron saint of the city – and its fair – after freeing it from the *Gargouille*; Saint-Patrice-et-Saint-Godard, which boasts Normandy's most beautiful stained-glass windows; the chapel of Corneille's secondary school; Saint-Nicaise, which combines Gothic and modern architecture; and the Madeleine, which is integrated into the classic-style buildings of the *Hôtel-Dieu*. Hugo referred to it as "The town of a hundred bells" after some of them had already disappeared. Before the French Revolution, Rouen had thirty-seven parishes and forty convents

Below
The Law Courts in Rouen, a jewel of civil architecture in the Norman capital and the pride of the people of Rouen.

Right page
The *Gros-Horloge* installed in 1527 in this arch overlooking Rouen's busiest and most visited street.

CREDIT LYONN
Tabacs

and priory, hospital and seminary chapels.

Built in 1970, the Church of Jeanne-d'Arc, located in *place du Vieux-Marché*, is the starting point of another Rouen tour which leads you in the footsteps of the famous shepherd girl of Domrémy. Designed by architect Louis Arrechte, the church, with its unusual uneven roof, is made of a wall of stained-glass windows that came from the Church of Saint-Vincent (destroyed during the 2nd World War), supported by a delicate concrete framework. In front of the sanctuary, below the *Galerie du Souvenir*, the base of the Saint-Sauveur pillars where a soldier went to fetch the crucifix requested by Joan of Arc, the pillory, the stones of the firewall and a small patch of land where the stake was driven into the ground, have been revealed. Topped by the tall Cross of Rehabilitation, these are moving evidence of the torture that Joan of Arc endured here on 30 May 1431. Other places in Rouen where her memory is honoured are 102 *rue Jeanne-d'Arc*, where she was imprisoned, the keep where she was threatened with torture, the Saint-Ouen gardens where she abjured, *rue Saint-Romain* where her rehabilitation process took place before the church officials and the Joan of Arc museum.

The Rouen people are very proud of their courthouse. Home to the seat of the Exchequer and the Parliament of Normandy, it was rebuilt between 1499 and 1543 and expanded several times. Its façades reveal the constant development of Gothic and Flamboyant art, with the design of their balustrades, pinnacles and the shape of their windows becoming lighter and more inventive the higher up they went. The main courtyard, under which an 11th-century synagogue was discovered, features a large staircase leading to the public prosecu-

Below

The entrance to the Rouen Fine Arts museum, one of the most beautiful museums in provincial France. A large area is dedicated to Géricault, David, Dufy and the Impressionists.

tors' room which is covered with a wainscoted wooden arch. It also leads to the Court of assizes with its "fearsome beauty" that so impressed the French historian Michelet.

The bell tower is another emblem of power and history. The Cache-Ribaude, one of its bells, peals each evening at 9 o'clock to sound the curfew as was decreed by William the Conqueror. It is one of the most visited monuments in Rouen, along with the adjacent arcade that bears the Gros-Horloge (Big Clock) which has been telling time to passers-by in the busiest street of Rouen since 1529.

Located on the banks of a river that links it to the sea and Paris, Rouen has always been an important market place, trading with the world at large. Opulent majestic façades tell of the affluence of its magistrates, cloth weavers, merchants and shipowners. Some examples are the *Hôtel Bourgtheroulde*, the *Bureau des Finances*, the *Hôtel Hocqueville* ceramics museum and the *Hôtel Etancourt*. However, the most original structures found in Rouen – to the point of irritating Stendhal – are its half-timbered houses. These houses were renovated after a period of neglect and currently add to the charm and picturesque quality of *rue Saint-Romain*, *rue de*

Above
Ceramics museum.

Right
A stele was erected to the memory of Gustave Flaubert, born in Rouen on 12 December 1821, in the museum named after him housed in the Hôtel-Dieu hospital.

Martainville, *rue Damiette*, *rue Eau-de-Robec* and *place du Vieux-Marché*.

A two-hour walk to the historic centre will have convinced you of its vast wealth. The ancient city has other assets apart from its architecture to delight you, such as its literary history for example. In Rouen, you can visit the family abode of the famous writer Pierre Corneille on *rue de la Pie* and the apartment of head surgeon and father of Gustave, Achille Flaubert at the Hôtel-Dieu hospital, whose monumental cemetery holds his tomb. The poet Saint-Amant, writer Jeanne-Marie Leprince de Beaumont, encyclopaedist Bernard de Fontenelle, playwright Armand Salacrou and novelist Maurice Leblanc were all born in Rouen. Maupassant, Gide, Alain, Maurois and Mac Orlan also lived there for long periods of time. If you are not convinced, just read what enthusiasts or critics such as the Marquise de Sévigné, Saint-Simon, Stendhal, Nodier, Michelet, Balzac, Hugo, Zola and Léautaud wrote about it.

Another of Rouen's assets is its museums. Three thousand paintings, seven thousand drawings and four hundred sculptures are on display at its Fine Arts museum whose most valued treasures include the works of Géricault, Gérard David, the Impressionists and Raoul Dufy. Ceramics, the art for which Rouen made a name for itself, with its use of blue and ochre backgrounds and rose decorations, has its own museum, the *Hôtel d'Hocqueville*, while the ironwork and locksmith trades have their place at the Le Secq-des-Tournelles museum in the old Church of Saint-Laurent. The Winged Stag tapestry and the *mosaïque de Lillebonne* are two of the most remarkable pieces to be found at the *Musée des Antiquités de la Seine-Maritime*. The neighbouring natural history museum holds 500,000 pieces that touch on Normandy's bird and wildlife history. At the Hôtel-Dieu hospital, the Flaubert museum is annexed by a medical history museum while the home of the four Aymon brothers houses the Education museum.

Rouen's harbours are also well worth a visit. The riverside harbour is the relay point between the sea and Paris but Rouen is also considered one of France's leading maritime harbours. Its trade is concentrated downstream of *pont Guillaume* where the docks, warehouses, grain silos and different infrastructures are located. Owing to development work along the river Seine which began as early as 1848, large vessels can moor head and stern along its wharves that stretch along the right bank to Val-de-la-Haye and the left bank to La Bouille, Tancarville and Honfleur. The maritime museum, next to the tide gauge station, and the guided tours will provide you with details of the harbour's activity.

The *Halle aux Toiles*, the *rue Verte* train station, the high *Vieille Tour*, the botanical gardens, the Fine-Arts theatre, in front of which Corneille was reputed to have recited verses of the *Cid*, and the Sainte-Marie fountain are some more of the remarkable monuments to be seen in this "museum town", which was described as "never-ending" by Jean de La Varende.

Right page
The ancient Church of Saint-Laurent was closed down and converted into an ironworks museum.

Below
Avenue Pasteur in Rouen (a recently renovated district). In the background, Sainte-Madeleine Church.

ROUEN AND ITS SURROUNDING AREA

The city of Rouen has a population of 100,000 while its surrounding area has about four times this figure. Since the 19th century, the textile, oil, chemistry, paper and automotive industries have transformed the local environment into a large industrial complex within the loop of the river Seine between Elbeuf and Moulineaux or the Robec, Cailly and Austreberthe valleys. But never fear, the countryside is a stone's throw from this universe of factories, cranes, motorways and freeways.

Three large forests, La Londe-Rouvray, the *Forêt Verte* and Roumare forest, where Rollo hung gold bracelets to test the honesty of his subjects, encircle Rouen and its surrounding area. These forests are places of significant historical interest.

Downstream of Elbeuf, also a Town of Art and History and a former major cloth manufacturing town, as portrayed in a stained-glass window, the chalk cliffs of Orival give this part of Normandy a Jurassic or Dolomitic appearance. On the other bank of the Seine lie the Saint-Adrien Rocks, a popular pilgrim destination.

To the east of Normandy's capital, the Château of Martainville, a magnificent 15th- and 17th-century residence, houses outstanding collections of furniture, crockery, utensils and costumes from the region's various areas. In Ry, a monument on the bank of the river Crevon and a robot museum pay tribute to Gustave Flaubert. This is said to be the village of Yonville-l'Abbaye where the plot of *Madame Bovary* unfolds.

Above

The Rouen wharf during the "Sails of freedom" gathering.

Right page

On the Moulineaux hillside stands the famous castle of Robert the Devil, a legendary character depicted in poems and novels who was perhaps inspired by Robert the Magnificent's enemies.

In Boos, the ceramic decorated dovecote belonged to the country estate of the Saint-Amand abbesses. The Basilica of Notre-Dame-de-Bonsecours is one of the many shrines to the Virgin Mary found in Normandy. In the past, a rack railway linked Rouen to this residential town that offers a remarkable panoramic view of the Seine valley from the cemetery where the poet Heredia is buried and its surroundings. In Darnétal in Carville, where the Church of Saint-Ouende-Paon and the tower of the Church of Saint-Pierre can be visited, a few of the many mills that kept Robec and Aubette alive have recovered some of their splendour.

Flaubert spent many nights awake writing his novels in a small lodge located in the corner of a garden, which is all that remains of the family property in Croisset. His bookcase is preserved by the town hall of Canteleu. André Marie, one of its mayors, who was a sculpture lover, placed the works of Rodin, Janiaux, Bourdelle, Gromaire and others in the streets of Barentin, thus creating a genuine outdoor museum.

Right
The Church of Orival, a rare example of a troglodytic church, which is partly buried under the cliff.

Below
The dovecote of the country house of the Saint-Amand abbesses, a large Rouen abbey, that disappeared when *rue de la République* was built in 1810.

Voltaire was a guest at the castle of La Rivière-Bourdet in Quevillon. On the left bank lies the town of La Bouille, the home town of Hector Malot, author of *Sans famille*, who was born here in 1830 and whose parents' house still stands here. It was the crossing point between Haute- and Basse-Normandie for centuries and remains a place for relaxation that is popular with the people of Rouen. On the hillside of Moulineaux above the remains of Robert the Devil's castle flies the Norman flag. This Robert was dreamt up by the populist novelists of the 19th century... unless this was slander on the part of Robert the Magnificent's enemies. The ancient fortress, built in the 11th century, is home to a Viking museum. In the woods and just under the castle, a monument known as the "Qui Vive" and dear to the writer André Maurois commemorates the resistance of the Norman *franc-tireurs* in 1870. In Petit-Couronne, a gate in the middle of the high walls leads to the country house of the playwright Pierre Corneille.

Top, right
The lodge of Croisset in Canteleu is all that remains of the Flaubert family property. The writer loved to relax and entertain his friends there and watch ships go up the river Seine.

Botton, right
A plaque commemorating receptions that were organised in Paris to mark the birthday of a great writer whose relations with Rouen were not always easy.

VAL DE SEINE

The river Seine flows along 110 miles from Rouen to Le Havre – or almost 50 miles as the crow flies - to meet up with the estuary. This lazy meandering course has created landscapes with Moulineaux, Bardouville, Hénouville, Duclair and Le Trait providing magnificent panoramic views. The course of the river can often be closely followed and is ideally explored during boat trips. In the spring, cherry and apple trees paint the scenery with pastel colours while in the autumn, the forests clothe the landscape with more vibrant colours. On its left bank, in Notre-Dame-de-Bliquetuit, an old farm houses the headquarters of the *Parc Naturel Régional des Boucles de la Seine*, which covers some of this area.

Mankind has been enjoying this spot for centuries. Five large abbeys are located here. Raoul de Tancarville, a Chamberlain of William the Conqueror, founded the collegiate church on which the Benedictines of Saint-Evroult built the abbey church dedicated to Saint George. This magnificent Romanesque building, whose surrounding French-style gardens have recently been restored, stands in the centre of the village of Saint-Martin-de-Boscherville. Its porch and façade are particularly outstanding. It has remained intact thanks to the locals who used it as their parish church during the French Revolution.

The neighbouring town of Jumièges was founded in 654 by Saint Philibert, destroyed by the Vikings then rebuilt by William Longsword. Two churches were built in succession, parallel to each other. Only the

Left page
The river Seine from the heights of Le Trait. "I saw all the beautiful spots and turns of this beautiful river Seine… Its banks are nothing like those of the Loire", said Marquise de Sévigné to Madame de Grignon.

Below
The magnificent Romanesque Abbey of Saint-George stands tall in the centre of the village of Saint-Martin-de-Boscherville.

two towers that surround the façade, the three level walls of the nave and part of the lantern tower supported by a huge arch remain of the Church of Notre-Dame. The porch and a few of the nave bays remain of the Church of Saint-Pierre while only a large storeroom, the chapter house and the sacristy of relics remain of the convent itself. When it came to choosing, the Jumièges parishioners decided to make Notre-Dame their parish church, but their priest was against the idea, deeming the upkeep, which had already ruined its religious community, to be too expensive. The priest ordered its destruction, preferring the 12th-century Church of Saint-Valentin, which was already the parish church. When the proud abbey was torn down, Saint-Valentin received some of its treasures, including stained-glass windows, statues and furniture. It is well worth a visit.

Jumièges Abbey, one of the largest Norman abbeys, is, according to the writer R. de Lasteyrie, "one of the most admirable ruins in France". The memory of Agnès Sorel, the mistress of Charles VII, lives on here. She died in the nearby *Manoir des Vignes* castle on 9 February 1450; she was supposedly struck down by puerperal fever but it is believed that she may actually have been poisoned. The *Dame de Beauté* now lies in Loches, but her heart and entrails were buried in Notre-Dame Church. Her black tombstone is one of the treasures of the small museum in the abbey house, where you can also see the recumbent statue of the *Enervés de Jumièges*, characters whose identity has been the subject of much controversy.

An acquaintance of King Dagobert founded the abbey that currently bears his name, Saint-Wandrille, in 649. This was originally known as the Abbey de la Fontenelle, after a stream which springs up here. Its Gothic church was also destroyed before Victor Hugo, with his famous words, was able to put an end to the destruction of so many monuments. The monastic buildings that can be entered by

Top of page
The Gothic church of the abbey founded in the 6th century by Saint Wandrille, a subject of King Dagobert, fell prey to vandals.

Opposite
The wall of the nave and the towers of Notre-Dame of Jumièges are the largest remains of the church that was consecrated in the presence of William the Conqueror in 1067.

the Jarente door, and which were built in the classical style of the 17th and 18th centuries, were preserved. Benedictines of the Strict Observance set up again here in 1931. Still in existence today, their community made the abbey a place of prayer and retreat which is also open to visitors in search of spiritual food. The tithe barn of La Neuville-du-Bosc, which was pulled down and rebuilt piece by piece, is currently its new church where the scull of Saint Wandrille lies in the reliquary near the chancel.

The abbeys of Gruchet-Valasse and Montivilliers are also located in Seine-Maritime among the Norman abbeys. These are to be found in the Lillebonne and Le Havre regions. Empress Matilda, William the Conqueror's granddaughter and wife of Geoffroy Plantagenet by a second marriage, founded the former of the two. The Plantagenet Coat of arms is engraved on the pediment of its monastic building which was built in the 18th century. In Montivilliers, the lantern tower and the north tower of the Church of Saint-Sauveur of a monastery founded in the 6th century by Saint Philibert testify to the importance of this historical place six centuries later.

According to Henry IV, the Church of Caudebec-en-Caux was the "the most beautiful chapel in the kingdom". Flamboyant art had reached its peak here as seen in its door, façade, bell tower, architecture and sculptures. The statuettes at the door (musician angels) and the balustrades running along the top of the nave or the base of the bell tower – reproducing the words of the Magnificat – are of particular interest.

Above
The Church of Caudebec-en-Caux, which according to Henry IV is "the most beautiful chapel in the kingdom".

On the inside, the suspended keystone of the Chapel of the Virgin Mary was a feat of Guillaume Le Tellier, the architect of the sanctuary who was buried under this vault. Beautiful walkways line the river Seine, which plays an important role in Caudebec where a museum is dedicated to river boating. A rare model of Templar houses can be seen in this lovely town which was greatly damaged during the 2nd World War. In the past, Caudebec was where people came to watch the tidal bore, a rare phenomenon since the various developments along the river Seine.

A short way off the Val de Seine route lies Yvetot, the capital of *Pays de Caux* country, which was the kingdom of a "little king" who was made famous by the French singer Béranger. The song of course has a historical basis: Yvetot indeed had a "king" up to the time of the French Revolution but his power, like his estate, was very limited. In addition to the *Musée des Ivoires* and the ANEth garden, the Church of Saint-Pierre is worth a visit when in Yvetot. With its rotunda shape and immense Max Ingrand stained windows for lighting, it reveals all too rare but delightful contemporary religious architecture. Near Yvetot, the Allouville oak tree, which is over a thousand years old, still thrives. With the chapel built by the parish priest in its trunk in 1696, it is one of Normandy's most unusual sights.

On 4 September 1843, Charles Vacquerie, a budding poet, and his young wife, Léopoldine Hugo, drowned while rowing on the river Seine after they were caught by surprise in a tidal bore. The memory of this tragedy forever marked the village of Villequier. Hugo expressed his pain in unforgettable verses:

I will relive this moment until
my dying day
The moment of useless tears!
Where I cried: the child that
I had a moment ago
Why is she no longer here
Don't be annoyed if I am what I am
Oh my God, this wound has been
sore for so long.

The family house of the Vacqueries, which was converted into a museum, holds souvenirs related to this tragic event, its victims and Victor Hugo's life.

Lillebonne is an important place in Norman history. Before the arrival of the Normans, for a long time it was only known as the site of the largest Gallo-Roman monument north of the Loire – its theatre. However, ducal history also has its place there. According to tradition, William the Conqueror gathered his vassals here to prepare the conquest of England and held a council of Norman prelates in 1082. However, the keep only dates back to the time of Philippe Auguste. Two museums and the theatre itself testify to the town's importance during the Gallo-Roman era as well as in the more recent past.

Tancarville, known as the place where the first bridge was built (in 1959) on the estuary, is also home to a tremendous castle, built in the woods above the river Seine. This castle doubled as a fortress and family dwelling. The Le Havre industrial estate starts at this point, and is crossed by the Tancarville canal. Ships pass through the Grand Canal in Le Havre to reach the estate.

The estate is a large industrial complex, particularly for the oil industry, where the 242-metre tall chimneys of the French electric company's thermal heating plant rise up like two giant lighthouses.

Below, left
The village of Villequier that preserves the memory of the tragedy that took place there on 4 September 1843.

Below, right
The bridge of Tancarville, which is the oldest structure crossing the estuary of the river Seine.

LE HAVRE

In September 1944, the Allied forces, misinformed about the number of German troops that still occupied the area, bombed and destroyed Le Havre again. The rebuilding of the town was assigned to architect Auguste Perret. An enthusiast of straight lines and wide open spaces and a pioneer of the use of reinforced concrete, he decided to plan the city based on the chequerboard design of the first town planner of Le Havre, the Italian Bellarmoto.

His work wasn't very popular with the masses and received much criticism. It gave Le Havre the reputation of being a cold and hard place of undeserved tourist interest. Time had left its mark on the existing structures so new buildings were built, spaces redesigned and old monuments restored. You will find Le Havre an interesting place if you are not expecting a city built to the mediaeval or "Norman" model. Le Havre is a World Heritage Site and the Perret apartment, a faithful reproduction of the one designed by the architectural genius in the 1950s, is a must-see.

Besides, Le Havre is a fairly recent city. It was founded in 1517 by François I and became the largest harbour in the kingdom. Honfleur was too small and Harfleur – a landing stage on the banks of the river Seine – was silting up. Incidentally, this pretty town on the mouth of the Lézarde, which was much praised by Hugo, features the tallest bell tower in Normandy. The site was chosen by the great French admiral, Bonnivet, due to the increasing size of vessels at the time and the fact that high tide lasted two full hours. Over time, "Havre de Grâce" then, "Françoise de Grâce" became Le Havre, Normandy's largest city in terms of population. Among its famous offspring are French writers Bernardin de Saint-Pierre, Casimir Delavigne and Raymond Queneau, the political scientist, André Siegfried, and the politician, René Coty.

There are three or four different towns – or layers – to Le Havre that can be visited simultaneously or alternately. Located not far from the *bassin du Roi* dock where the royal vessel *Hermine*, the first ship ever to dock in this harbour, came to moor in 1518, the Saint-François district bears witness to the first town, with its former Law Courts, now home to the Natural History Museum, and the *Maison de l'Armateur*, an 18th-century dwelling with a stunning octagonal central light shaft. Notre-Dame Cathedral also belongs to this era but the cabled ionic columns standing before the north gate and the west façade that decorate this structure, combining both Gothic and Renaissance styles, never cease to amaze. In the immediate surroundings, the Abbey church of Graville, which was dedicated to the 4th-century martyr

Above

From the *bassin du Commerce*, spanned by an elegant footbridge, two of the most outstanding buildings in Le Havre today can be admired: the "Volcano", in the foreground, and the bell tower of Saint-Joseph Church.

Saint Honorine, testifies to a past that dates back well before the birth of Le Havre, because it was built in the 12th century. A museum was set up in the monastic buildings and dedicated to the two themes of sacred art and houses throughout the ages. The streets that lead up to the fort of Sainte-Adresse, the *Pain de Sucre* hill, Notre-Dame-des-Flots chapel, the fort of Tourneville and the upper town of Le Havre evoke a little of the atmosphere of the pre-war town.

Avenue Foch epitomises the rebuilt city. Its long avenue is wider than the Champs-Elysées and it is also lined with shaded walkways and runs between two long lines of buildings of superb architectural unity. It passes in front of the city hall and the landscaped square in the foreground, which is the biggest in Europe. At the end of the avenue stand two tall towers, which symbolise the "Ocean gateway", the beautiful name given to Le Havre. In the middle of the rebuilt districts, like those of the great Norman sanctuaries, stands the 109-metre tall octagonal tower of Saint-Joseph Church. Audigier, its architect, adopted the idea from Auguste Perret. He designed this church as a large square nave, placing the high altar in its centre at the base of the lantern tower, which is 90m high and supported by four pillars. He also thought of lighting up the sanctuary with 12,768 translucent panels stained with fifty different colours that were to be inserted into the concrete of the tower and the nave, providing ever-changing light.

In the centre of Le Havre, the water of the *bassin du Commerce* dock spanned by the elegant metal footbridge is mainly used by novice sailors. The *Palais de la Bourse* trading centre, one of the oldest in France, was built on these wharves but its offices are now home to the casino. To the west, along the extension of this dock, lies the Espace Niemeyer (named after its Brazilian architect), which is Le Havre's main arts centre. The "Volcano", a tall white structure shaped like a cruise liner's smokestack, houses theatres, cinemas and seminar and conference facilities. Built in 1960 at the water's edge and not far from the signal station, the Malraux museum became famous for its architecture and collections. The light quality that bathes

Below
The beach at Sainte-Adresse, a residential area on the outskirts of Le Havre, at nightfall. Its cliffs provide a spectacular view over the sea. It was the seat of the Belgian Government in 1914-1918.

the rooms particularly accentuates the works of artists Raoul Dufy (born in Le Havre), Boudin, Monet, Renoir, Millet and Flemish and Dutch masters whose works are exhibited there. The museum looks right out onto the sea. The concrete sculpture in front of its glass façade is a fitting depiction of the activities that take place here. Its name is "The Eye".

For a long time, the harbour of Le Havre – whose *Conservatoire maritime*, based in a hangar of the former transatlantic station, traces the harbour's history and preserves its heritage – was a place of dreams. It was the era when the prestigious cruise liners, the America-bound *Normandie*, *Liberté* and *France*, could be seen on its wharves. The arrival of the aeroplane destroyed the dream. The ferries that currently leave the harbour terminal head for England or Ireland. It is the traffic of goods and container ships that make the oil harbour of Le Havre and Antifer, where 32 million tonnes of crude oil were docked in 2002, one of the leading oil harbours in Europe. The 2 mile-long Port 2000, its most recent addition which was developed to environmental conservation standards, should help to maintain its rank. It is protected by 5 miles of dykes and its infrastructures stretch as far as Tancarville over 22,000 hectares of land. Some of these, such as the François I lock, beat world records with their size. You can end a tour of this site (a "must" when in Le Havre) with a stroll to the end of the north jetty. No storm hits France without us getting a picture of the onslaught of its lighthouse being lashed by huge waves. When the sea calms, we can almost touch the big ships that have come from far and wide or that are about to leave. In the hinterland, some châteaux stand on the *Pays de Caux* plateau, like tiny islands in the rolling fields: Orcher, whose grounds form terraces rising above the Seine; Le Val d'Arques, in Saint-Eustache-la-Forêt; La Petite-Croix, whose pink brick walls used to house the musician André Caplet; Filières, in Gommerville; and Gourdemare, a typical *Pays de Caux* residence in Manneville-la-Goupil.

Above

Near to the entrance of the harbour and the signal station lies the André-Malraux museum, with the sculpture named "The Eye" in front of its façade.

THE ALABASTER COAST

Eighty miles of cliffs line the *pays de Caux* with their white, clay and flint streaked walls that have been exposed to erosion over time. Like at Cape Fagnet, these cliffs are sometimes higher than 100 metres. When wall sections fall into the sea, they dissolve and colour the sea and as a result, the shoreline has become known as the Alabaster Coast. The famous town of Etretat, Yport, Veulettes, Veules-les-Roses, Saint-Aubin and Sainte-Marguerite are among the many seaside towns that have extended their beaches into the coves. Along this coast, sailors have found a mere handful of sites for casting their anchor. These are no other than the famous harbours of Fécamp, Saint-Valery-en-Caux, Dieppe and Le Tréport. The French electric company set up two nuclear power plants in Penly and Paluel.

You might have difficulty locating the Alabaster Coast but you can't miss Etretat. The pebbles, "doors" and "needles" make it one of those sites that we seem to know without ever visiting. On both sides of the "riprap", the dyke trail that overlooks the beach, stand the *Aval* cliff to the west and the *Amont* cliff to the north. Like a cathedral on its buttresses, the *Aval* cliff appears to be held up by the arch that erosion created between its peak and the sea, while facing it at barely a cable's length away, stands the giant rock of the "Hollow" needle, 70 metres high. Beyond lies the *Manneporte* (invisible from the beach) which can be seen from the footpath that runs along the top of the *Aval* cliff and which opens up like the giant porch of a new sanctuary with the sea pounding below. Towards the east, above a third and much smaller "door" stretches the jagged line of the *Amont* cliff ridges where the bell tower and roof of the Notre-Dame-de-la-Garde chapel can be made out.

It was the artist Isabey who in the 19th century discovered Etretat, a fishing village in the hollow of a parched valley. A few thatch roof houses surrounded the church, its lantern tower and its Romanesque porch and in the evening, the fishermen hauled their skiffs (small boats) to the top of the beach. The artists Corot, Jongkind, Courbet and Monet later joined or followed him. Then came musicians such as Offenbach and Massenet and writers, such as Maupassant, followed by the great people of this world. Alphonse Karr,

Bottom, left
Among other things, Etretat cultivates the memory of Guy de Maupassant, one of its first loyal visitors.

Below
A few skiffs, the vessels of Etretat fishermen in the past, lie on the pebble beach.

who invented the trend of tourist destinations, saw to the "promoting" of Etretat, which at the end of the 19th century became the favourite Normandy haunt of artists and high society people. Maurice Leblanc rendered it famous by making the "Hollow" needle the refuge of his hero, the gentleman thief Arsène Lupin. Obviously the "needle" wasn't hollow but nothing beats a grain of mystery at making this site successful and besides, other legendary characters had already lived there, like in the neighbouring cliffs of *Emeraude* and *Blanche Ecume* and their caves.

A Belle Epoque aura floats around Etretat, submerged in a sea of hydrangea bouquets on its hotels, villas, houses and *Vieux Marché* (Old market), which was built in 1926. The castle of Aygues, home of the composer Offenbach then the Queens of Spain, the *Clos Arsène Lupin*, home of author Maurice Leblanc and the *villa Orphée* of the composer Massenet, are all souvenirs of the past there.

On the *Amont* cliff stands a large white arrow monument pointing towards the horizon in commemoration of the pilots Nungesser and Coli. Their plane was seen here for the last time during their Atlantic crossing attempt in 1927.

In the surrounding area, the lighthouse of Antifer, built on a cliff that towers 102 metres above sea level, and the needle of Belval, are two popular spots for walks near Etretat. The more literary minded might want to head for Cuverville whose castle was the home of André Gide and his wife. The author of *Strait is the Gate* and *The Immoralist* lies in the little cemetery in the chevet of the church.

Above

Saint Valéry-en-Caux harbour, a shelter on the Alabaster Coast.

FÉCAMP

Does Fécamp owe its fame to fishing or to the "Palace" where the famous liqueur matures?

A town of art and history, Fécamp has many strings to its bow.

As is often the case, there is a legend behind Fécamp's origins. It all started with the trunk of a fig tree (*ficus* in Latin) washed up on its shores and containing a few drops of Precious Blood.

In 658, a monastery was founded on this relic but two hundred years later the Vikings massacred its nuns and destroyed its walls. William Longsword, son of Rollo, rebuilt it and Richard I, his son, turned it into a Benedictine abbey whose church was consecrated in 990.

After it was set on fire by lightning, it was rebuilt in the 12th century, and restructured in the 15th and 18th centuries.

Its lantern tower and nave almost measure up to those of Notre-Dame in Paris.

Inside, the statues, bas-reliefs, cenotaphs and liturgical objects that make the *Trinité* such a masterpiece also illustrate the miracles that took place at the sanctuary and in Fécamp. A reliquary contains the footprint of the Archangel Saint Michael, who ordered the bishops to dedicate the sanctuary to the Holy Trinity. Leaning against the chancel is a tabernacle of white marble containing the relic of the Precious Blood that arrived in the trunk of the fig tree. In the Sacré-Cœur chapel lies William of Volpiano, who was called to the head of the *Trinité* in 1003 and who returned and died in 1031. He ensured that this monastery had equal prestige to that of the Mont-Saint-Michel abbey. Richard I "the Fearless" and his son Richard II "the Good" were also buried here. The town hall is set in the monastic buildings.

Fécamp's inhabitants had been cod fishing in Newfoundland since the 16th century and carried on this "great trade" up until the 1970s. Miniature models, rebuilt boats, paintings, pictures, figureheads, old tools and equipment at the *Terre-Neuvas* museum take us back to the years when long-range and herring fishing and ship building made Fécamp a thriving, prosperous town. On the cliff, the Church of Notre-Dame-du-Salut is still a popular site for pilgrims and a landmark for sailors.

Below

Nowadays sailing adds life to the docks and wharves of the longtime great cod- and herring-fishing harbour of Fécamp.

The Benedictine Palace is the most visited place in Fécamp and one of the most popular in Normandy. It was built in 1888 by the Fécamp industrialist Alexander the Great, who was determined and imaginative and an avant-garde genius in advertising. It was rebuilt in 1893 after being engulfed by fire and has a mediaeval appearance with its bell tower, campanile, windows and elaborately decorated balustrades.

Such was the desire of its founder and architect Camille Albert who imitated Gothic and Renaissance architecture in an Art Nouveau spirit. After a tour of the Benedictine Palace, you can taste the liqueur invented by Alexander the Great from a health potion that was prepared in 1510 by a Fécamp monk, Bernardo Vincelli, whose book of spells was found by the industrialist. Although its secret recipe includes herbs gathered in the meadows and neighbouring cliffs, it includes others, twenty-seven in all, that botanists are not accustomed to finding there, such as vanilla, nutmeg, hyssop and cinnamon, but which already existed during the Renaissance period. The Palace not only offers delights for food-lovers and an insight into the manufacture and history of the subtle and delightful liqueur. It also reveals the stills with their copper-coloured reflections and the oak barrels where the liqueur is made and matured. Its rooms hold numerous works from the Middle Ages and the Renaissance period such as manuscripts, statues, illuminations, ivory, alabaster and ironwork pieces belonging to Alexander the Great – an avid collector who enjoyed sharing his discoveries with the public. A room is also dedicated to the work of artists who were to become famous, like Miro, Niki de Saint Phalle and Braque before them.

Right
The lantern tower of the *Trinité* in Fécamp, which is almost as tall as the towers of Notre-Dame in Paris.

Below
Built and rebuilt in the Gothic and Renaissance style after a fire at the end of the 19th century, the Benedictine Palace is a famous historical site for food-lovers and a remarkable culture centre.

Above

Among the tombs of the marine cemetery that surrounds the Church of Varengeville, you can kneel before the tombs of Georges Braque, Albert Roussel or Georges Porto-Riche.

PAYS DE CAUX COUNTRY

Two routes link Fécamp to Dieppe. One runs along the coast and the other weaves its way through *Pays de Caux* country.

On the first route, the most interesting town is Varengeville-sur-Mer. The marine cemetery surrounding the Chapel of Saint-Valery, the manor of the powerful shipowner of the Renaissance period, Ango, and the *Bois des Moustiers* and Shamrock parks all add to the appeal of this town for many different reasons. The second more winding route crosses gentler *Pays de Caux* country than that described by Maupassant, land which is turned a wonderful shade of blue in

Opposite

The Château de Cany, built at the end of the Louis XIII period, is surrounded by moats fed by the River Durdent.

June by linen, a typical crop in the area. Around Goderville, the farms with their dilapidated houses, or *cours masures*, still provide protection from the wind with their high mounds of earth and curtains of trees.

Below
The manor of Ango, a powerful shipowner and financier of the Renaissance period and friend of François I, who died a pauper. The brick decoration on the dovecote is of particular interest.

The road invites visitors to wander from castle to castle: from Valmont, birthplace of a great Norman family, the Estouvilles, where the Benedictines revived the Abbey of Notre-Dame-du-Pré, to Sassetot-le-Mauconduit, which welcomed Empress Elisabeth "Sissi"; from Cany-Barville, a uniform example of the Louis XIII style, to Oherville, where the *Manoir d'Auffay* houses the *Musée des colombiers cauchois*; from Ecretteville-lès-Baons, whose *Manoir du Câtel* is one of the oldest in Normandy, to Doudeville, where the steps of a certain Maréchal de Villars still resound; from Crasville-la-Roquefort to Saint Pierre-le-Vieux; from Longueville-sur-Scie to Ouville-la-Rivière. In Grainville-la-Teinturière, a museum retraces the surprising epic of the village's lord who conquered the Canary Islands in 1402, proclaimed himself King and came back to the village where he ended his adventurous life as a pauper.

ARQUES-LA-BATAILLE

On the doorstep of Dieppe, the castle of Tourville-sur-Arques could merely owe its fame to the name of its first owner, Thomas Hue, the Marquis of Miromesnil. For we surely owe the beginnings of the abolition of torture to this minister of Louis XVI. Sometimes history is very unfair.

It is more likely, however, that the birth of Guy de Maupassant on 5 August 1850 within its walls was the reason behind the fame of this beautiful 17th-century dwelling, rented at the time by the parents of the future novelist who lived there for just three years. The fortress that stands on a narrow headland where

Above
Standing proudly above the river Béthune, the citadel of Arques-la-Bataille was the stage of great episodes in Normandy's and France's history.

Below
The castle of Miromesnil, in Tourville-sur-Arques, birthplace of Guy de Maupassant.

Below
The postern of Arques fortress is decorated with a bas-relief celebrating Henry IV who won a decisive battle against the leaguers of the Duke of Guise on 21 September 1589.

the Varenne and the Béthune rivers meet is almost one thousand years old. In 1054, William the Conqueror attacked William the Count of Arques there but it was Henry I Beauclerc then François I who gave it its true importance. Philippe Auguste and Charles the Reckless besieged it in vain, Talbot and Warwick with success. However, the most famous battle that was fought there was that of 1589 where Henry IV was victorious over the leaguers... The citadel, whose walls seem to defy the laws of balance, sometimes served as a prison. Eleanor of Brittany and Joan of Arc were held in its dungeons.

Below and right
The 15th-century castle, which was home to Dieppe's governors and where Chateaubriand had a garrison, today houses a rare precious ivory collection.

DIEPPE

The castle terrace to the west and the heights of Pollet, once a picturesque district of sailors and fishermen, to the east, both give a view of Dieppe that should not be missed: Dieppe, a sub-prefecture of Seine-Maritime, leisurely spreads out over the area provided by the *Deep* (an estuary of the river Arques).

Is this where sea bathing all began? Of this we are quite certain. It is said to have been started in 1824 by the Duchess of Berry. Vast green spaces and a wide avenue overlook the beach which was home to this historical sea bathing site. Dieppe sea front, which is just over a mile long, is one of the most pleasant beaches you may ever come across. Every year, kite-flying lovers from all over the world meet up here.

Dieppe played a key role in the discovery of the world by sea and in the fight against Portugal's claims on Africa. Jean de Béthencourt, Jean

Above
Lively Dieppe harbour, which served as a stopover point on the way to England, boasted a large fishing fleet and played a key role in the discovery of the world by sea.

Cousin, Raoul and Jean Parmentier, Verrazano and Champlain all sailed from this harbour, heading for Sumatra and New York, among others. In the Church of Saint-Jacques, the sculpted motifs of the "*Frise des Sauvages*" illustrate the meeting of captains and people of distant lands. Jean Ango, the great shipowner and friend of François I, who financed these expeditions and died a pauper, was buried there.

After it was destroyed by an Anglo-Dutch fleet in 1694, Dieppe was rebuilt to the plans of one of Vauban's deputies called Vertraben, but it never regained its former glory or its rank as Normandy's leading harbour. Also, some years earlier, the revocation of the Edict of Nantes led to the exile of some of its population. Dieppe has preserved some beautiful houses with colourful and white brick façades and beautiful ironwork balconies from its first reconstruction period. During the last war, its beaches and those of neighbouring towns such as Pourville, Sainte-Marguerite and Berneval staged the jubilee operation on 19 August 1942, a landing that paved the way for that of 1944.

In this war, the city was damaged and nearly 2,000 Allied soldiers died there, many of whom were Canadian. This event strengthened the ties that already existed between the Norman city and Canada whose emblem, stamped with a maple leaf, flies in numerous parts of the town.

The sea is still at the core of Dieppe's trade. It drew numerous artists, such as Renoir, Monet, Pissarro and Emile Blanche. Its harbour, which is linked to that of Newhaven, is still used for a large proportion of maritime traffic with England. Dieppe also dedicated a science and technology centre to the sea, the *Estran*, where four of its departments present different aspects of sea or ocean life and the fifth is home to spectacular aquariums.

For a long time and up until its trade was banned, Dieppe was an ivory capital. In addition to other exhibits, the museum set in the castle which was the former dwelling of the governors has a large collection of *objets d'art* that were made from this material, including statuettes, fans, clocks, crucifixes and navigation instruments.

Opposite
The Estran or *Cité de la Mer* (City of the Sea) is an interesting culture and science centre dedicated to the sea.

LE TRÉPORT AND EU

Le Tréport, the most northern seaside town of the Alabaster Coast, was nicknamed the "beach of Paris" because of its proximity to the capital. Regardless of the season, the fishing harbour wharves, the market place where the *Croix du Moustoir* stands, and the busy shopping streets are always bustling with life. The Church of Saint-Jacques, built on a shoulder of the cliff, and especially the remarkable keystones of the nave, date back to the 16th century.

A 378-step stairway and a funicular railway, doubtless the only one in Normandy, built in 1908 and recently restored, lead from the town centre to the *Calvaire des Terrasses* at the top of the cliff. From Ailly cape you can see as far as Crotoy, and from the base of the peak you can make out the rooftops of Le Tréport, the Bresle estuary and the seaside town of Mers-les-Bains... in Picardy.

A few kilometres upstream, Eu, recognised as the last remaining royal estate in France, is one of the Norman towns with the longest known history and, considering the size of the town today, the richest architectural heritage.

The vast château, whose façade blocks the landscape of the valley, was the preferred home of Louis-Philippe, before later becoming a favoured residence of the Count of Paris. The final King of France welcomed Queen Victoria on two occasions, and it was in Eu that the *Entente Cordiale* was concluded. He undertook the last major renovations of the château, whose construction

Below
The chevet of the collegiate Church of Saint-Laurent-O'Toole in Eu.

was begun by Catherine de Clèves in 1578 before being completed by Mlle de Montpensier. Louis-Philippe also introduced exotic species into the park, which can be seen among the magnificent beech trees – some of which are several hundred years old – that are the main feature of the grounds. The city was established well before this period, however. The remains of a major Gallo-Roman city have been restored and are on display in Le Bois l'Abbé. It was in Eu that Rollo, founder of Normandy, died in 932, and that William the Conqueror married Matilda of Flanders in 1053, even if these events have left no tangible mark. On the tomb of Laurent O'Toole, the Irish primate who died here when he came to plead the cause of his people to the King of England, a collegiate church was built and dedicated to him. Viollet-le-Duc, who restored this sanctuary, said of it: "I've never seen anything more beautiful." Its chancel, transept and original tower were destroyed by lightning in 1486 and have been rebuilt in a Flamboyant style in vivid contrast to the Gothic style of the nave. The statuary is outstanding, including a representation of Christ in sorrow and the Virgin bearing the effigy of Notre-Dame d'Eu. In the crypt, Louis-Philippe assembled the tombs and remains of the members of the Artois family.

The 16th and 17th century left the town with the fine group of buildings which form the *Hôtel-Dieu*, its chapel, chapter house, remarkable covered cemetery and the chapel of the *Lycée Anguier*, named after the four great sculptors who created this masterpiece of art and history. Gissay, Guillain, Nicolas and Tremblay together sculpted the fine cenotaph which stands in the white marble, that of Henri de Guise le Balafré, assassinated in Blois in 1588, and his wife, Catherine de Clèves.

Eu, a Town of Art and History, is today the capital of the glass industry, a product for which the Bresle valley is renowned. Almost 80% of the world's trademark bottles are still made there.

Left, top
Nicknamed the "beach of Paris", Le Tréport naturally features a casino.

Left, bottom
Behind the statue of Louis-Philippe, whose favourite residence was the immense castle of Eu.

PAYS DE BRAY COUNTRY

The castle of Mesnieres-en-Bray is the architectural wonder of *Pays de Bray* country. The vast dwelling flanked with defence towers that were merely for decorative purposes was built in the 15th century by Luc de Boissey. It is a masterpiece of the Renaissance period, but the monumental fan-shaped staircase that leads to the main courtyard only dates back to the 18th century. The *Galerie des Cerfs* (Stag gallery), the card room and the two chapels are the highlights of any castle tour.

The *Pays de Bray* country's charm lies in its natural surroundings and the quality of its produce. Its reputation is less showy but the *bondon de Neufchâtel* cheese (square, cylindrical or heart-shaped) is the oldest of Norman cheeses. It has been manufactured since 1035. It is also in Ferrières-en-Bray that the *petit-suisse* and the *carré frais* that Charles Gervais started to manufacture industrially were invented.

A deep gash caused by erosion of the plateau of Caux – the "button hole" of *Pays de Bray* country – is a geological wonder of which there are beautiful views from Beauvoir-en-Lyons, La Ferté-Saint-Samson and Bures-en-Bray. This land, murmuring with water, from where the Epte, Andelle, Béthune and Eaulne rivers spring up and diverge, is grove country, but the forest of Eawy is renowned along with that of Lyons as the most beautiful beech grove in France. In a straight line stretching almost 9 miles, the *allée des Limousins* (French oak) walkway is an impressive stretch of vegetation. Under its foliage, in Val Vigot, the Germans had constructed a V 1 launch pad, whose remains are now a place of remembrance. The gardens of Bellevue in Beaumont-le-Hareng, where the Himalayan poppy grows under the Norman skies, and Auffay, home to Bosmelet castle and the collegiate church with its famous *Tour des Jacquemarts*, are other interesting botanical and heritage sites.

The park of Montalent, Andelle lake and the woods of Epinay provide a fairytale setting in Forges-les-Eaux where the chalybeate and radioactive springs first benefited Louis XIII, Anne of Austria and Cardinal Richelieu and whose casino, one of the finest in France, is housed in an old Capuchin convent.

Should we also include the castle of Clères located on Rouen's doorstep as part of the *Pays de Bray*? Since 1919, millions of bird lovers have gathered under its trees and alongside its lawns where pink flamingos, cranes, swans and other birds, both exotic and domestic, live in relative freedom.

Left page
Louis XIII, Anne of Austria, and Cardinal Richelieu made the waters of Forges-les-Eaux famous. This is a site that really deserved a statue.

Opposite, right
This strong tower, flanking the façade of the castle of Mesnières, gives it a military appearance a little like a fortress.

Opposite, left
The *bondon de Neufchâtel* cheese, here in the shape of a heart, is taken as the ancestor of all Norman cheeses.

Table of contents

SOUVENIRS
LES MARAIS

Acknowledgements

We would like to thank the following Tourist Boards for the documentation they provided us with:

COMITÉ DÉPARTEMENTAL DU TOURISME DU CALVADOS
8 rue Renoir, 14000 Caen
Tel.: 02 31 27 90 30/Email: cdt@cg14.fr

COMITÉ DÉPARTEMENTAL DU TOURISME DE LA MANCHE
Maison du Département, 50008 Saint-Lô Cedex
Tel.: 02 33 05 98 70/Email: manchetourisme@cg50.fr

COMITÉ DÉPARTEMENTAL DU TOURISME DE L'ORNE
86 rue Saint-Blaise, BP 50, 61002 Alençon Cedex
Tel.: 02 33 28 88 71/Email: info@ornetourisme.com

COMITÉ DÉPARTEMENTAL DU TOURISME DE L'EURE
3 rue du Commandant-Letellier, BP 367,
27003 Evreux Cedex
Tel.: 02 32 62 04 27/Email: info@cdt-eure.fr

COMITÉ DÉPARTEMENTAL DU TOURISME DE SEINE-MARITIME
6 rue Couronné, BP 60, 76240 Bihorel
Tel.: 02 35 12 10 10
Email: seinemaritime.tourisme@wanadoo.fr

Editor: Christian Ryo
Graphic design and layout: Nord Compo, Villeneuve d'Ascq (59)
Editorial coordination: Caroline Decaudin
Cartography: Patrick Mérienne
Photoengraving: Micro Lynx, Rennes (35)
Printing: Pollina, Luçon (85) - L68515

ISBN 978-2-7373-4370-4 - Publisher no.: 5553.06.01.04.14
Legal deposit: January 2008. Printed in France.